Bundt Cake
BLISS

Delicious Desserts
FROM MIDWEST KITCHENS

SUSANNA SHORT

Foreword by Dotty Dalquist

MINNESOTA HISTORICAL SOCIETY PRESS

Cover photo by Eric Mortenson, Minnesota Historical Society

Design: Percolator Graphic Design, Minneapolis

www.mhspress.org

The Minnesota Historical Society Press is a member of the Association of American University Presses.

Manufactured in the United States of America

10 9 8 7 6 5 4 3 2

∞ The paper used in this publication meets the minimum requirements of the American National Standard for Information Sciences—Permanence for Printed Library Materials, ANSI Z39.48-1984.

Bundt® is the registered trademark of Northland Aluminum Products.

International Standard Book Number
ISBN 13: 978-0-87351-585-6 (paper)
ISBN 10: 0-87351-585-4 (paper)

Library of Congress Cataloging-in-Publication Data
Short, Susanna, 1966–
    Bundt cake bliss : delicious desserts from Midwest kitchens / Susanna Short.
        p. cm.
Includes index.
    ISBN-13: 978-0-87351-585-6 (pbk. : alk. paper)
    ISBN-10: 0-87351-585-4 (pbk. : alk. paper)
    1. Cake. 2. Cookery, American—Midwestern style. I. Title.
TX771.S4177 2007
641.8′653—dc22   2007008090

This book is for my mom, who taught me how to cook, and for Betsy, Mattie, and Henry— my three favorite people to cook for!

ACKNOWLEDGEMENTS

I want to thank the good people at Macalester-Plymouth United Church in St. Paul, Minnesota, and the Randall Davey Audubon Center in Santa Fe, New Mexico, for tasting more Bundts than I can count. A special thanks to Alice Short, Marie Foss, Janet Daub, Clara Short, Anne Kaplan, Mary Davis, Kim Bayer, Barbara Hettle, Erin Ferguson, and Florence Shaller, talented bakers who generously gave me recipes, love, and support. Thanks to Marilyn Ziebarth, my editor with the Minnesota Historical Society Press, who magically turned my passion and ideas into a book. I am especially appreciative of Greg Britton, director of the Minnesota Historical Society Press, for his trust and encouragement. My deep gratitude and abiding love go to Betsy Daub, my partner of fifteen years, for her editing, proofreading, and constant support.

Contents

Recipes

Glazes, Frostings, and Sauces

And the Bundt was Born!

DOROTHY "DOTTY" DALQUIST

These days, pretty much everybody knows about Bundt cakes. Baby boomers across the country grew up on them, and many of their children and grandchildren are enjoying these tasty creations. But that wasn't always the case.

Most people don't know that the home of the famous pan is right here in the Midwest. In 1950 two women on a fundraising venture for the Minneapolis chapter of the Hadassah Society approached my husband, H. David Dalquist, about manufacturing a tubular cast-iron cake pan similar to the pan used to bake *bundkuchen,* popular German coffeecakes. At that time we were expanding our small family business to include bakeware products, so the idea of creating a fresh take on the classic but reportedly hard-to-find European pan was intriguing. My gracious husband Dave, along with our engineer Don Nygren, spearheaded the design and metal work to create a cast-aluminum pan in our foundry.

The new and improved heavy cast-aluminum pan was circular and fluted, allowing the deliciously rich cake batter to bake and rise uniformly. Dave named our pan "Bundt," after the bundkuchen, which translates as a cake for a gathering of people. But an instant hit the Bundt was not. It took a lot of hard work and even more determination to get the American public hooked on the wonders of this special cake.

For years we attempted to sell Bundt pans without much success, and we even periodically entertained the idea of discontinuing the pan from our product line. Back then, we did all of our correspondence by letters, so you can imagine the time and effort it took to properly promote the pan and recipes. It was not until daily newspapers began featuring recipes for delicious cakes baked in the Bundt pan that sales began to pick up. Homemakers soon learned of the simplicity and creativity that the pan allowed, and buzz began building for the Bundt. This was an exciting and hectic time, as our family's kitchen served as a test kitchen, and our relatives and friends faithfully tried more cake recipes for us than one can ever imagine. We also brought freshly baked cakes into

1

our factory lunchrooms for our employees to enjoy and often boxed extras for food kitchens.

Finally, in 1966, the Bundt pan got its big break when a Texan named Ella Helfrich took second place in the 17th Annual Pillsbury Bake-Off with her fabulous Bundt cake recipe, Tunnel of Fudge. This delicious cake looked impressive, tasted irresistible, and was very easy to prepare. Pillsbury was soon flooded with more than 200,000 queries from bakers wanting to know where they could find our one-of-a-kind pan. Bundt pans began flying off store shelves.

As our business gained momentum, we frequently hosted gatherings for business clients on our Lake Superior boat. What better way to promote this popular pan than by serving a warm Bundt cake, freshly baked in our galley oven as we traversed those beautiful waters. I baked and demonstrated the many flavors of cakes that could be prepared in our pan—all easily accomplished with additions such as fruit, chocolate, cinnamon, dates, and raisins. On one particular weekend, when we hosted marketing executives from Pillsbury, the idea for special Bundt cake mixes was born. The deal was sealed when the executives hopped off the boat at the dock.

Today there are more than 60 million Bundt pans in households across the United States. Our family business, Nordic Ware, has grown into the leading manufacturer of bakeware.

Many people have fond memories of baking beautiful and delicious Bundts with their families and friends. What better way to rekindle cherished traditions— or to start your own—than by baking from the brilliant range of recipes in *Bundt Cake Bliss*. Fruits, chocolate chips, spices, nuts, puddings—all create unique flavors in these delicious recipes. As Susanna Short reveals, the ideas are endless and the end results are spectacular. The best part about the Bundt cake? If it isn't eaten on the first day, it tastes better the next, like good ol' home cooking!

Welcome to the wonderful world of Bundt!

Introduction

The Bundt has solved one of life's troublesome dilemmas: How does the ordinary person make a cake that is worth a second glance and also good to eat?

It's your mother's birthday. You pore over fancy cookbooks, selecting a cake recipe requiring two engineers, six pans, two ingredients you cannot pronounce, a spreadsheet, and the weekend. But that's okay; you really love your mother. So, you sweat and fuss and toil, and when you feast your eyes on the final product, you realize you have three choices:

- Purchase an unclaimed cake at the bakery—never mind that your mom's name isn't Norman and she didn't just retire!

- Whisper to your guests that your eight-year-old made the dessert, but since she's shy, it's best not to mention it.

- Throw out the cake and exclaim, "Mom, I love you so much I refuse to clog your arteries on this special day. Here, have a Honey Crisp apple."

Let's face it—rarely can most people make a round, perfectly layered cake that looks like the gorgeous pictures in the cookbooks. We end up disappointed, with creations that would please a young child but that adults are embarrassed to serve.

What about sheet cakes? Sheet cakes are easy, right? But the sheet cake says, "I love you enough to bake you a cake . . . *almost.*"

Bundt to the rescue! This remarkable pan reliably makes a moist, delicious cake—practically idiot-proof—that can be dressed up or down depending on your taste or the occasion. And, it's beautiful! Tall and round as a cake should be. As deftly formed as a pastry chef might create. Best of all is its classic Bundt shape, with its wide–narrow–wide flutes, ready-made slicing ridges, that satisfy the gluttons and dieters among us.

How does a Bundt work? The pan's shape permits the baker to simply pour or spoon the batter into a container that creates the sought-after tall, round dessert. But a standard tall, round pan by itself would never work—the cake would be too thick to be completely cooked at the center. Thus, the ingenious hole in the middle, which enables the cake to cook from the "inside" as well as the outside. It is an Everywoman's and Everyman's pan, turning first-time and nervous bakers into accomplished cooks. It says, "I am for you. Fear not!" And it is why so many people adore and use the pans.

Dozens of elaborate and lovely shapes are now available: Rose Bundt, Bavaria Bundt, Star Bundt, Cathedral Bundt, Mini-Bundt, Elegant Heart Bundt. Each consistently creates gorgeous cakes that impress and please.

Bundt. The name comes from the German "bund cake," a cake for a gathering of people. To successfully trademark the name, H. David Dalquist, the inventor of the Bundt pan, added a "t" to its name. In a way this mirrored the frequent spelling changes in the names of the immigrants who carried the pan's Central European ancestor, the *kugelhopf,* to America in the early 1900s.

The Bundt pan might have stayed a kugelhopf pan, were it not for Rose Joshua and Fannie Schanfield, women from Minneapolis who longed for the rich and heavy cakes of their heritage. Sometime in the late 1940s, Rose Joshua arrived at Fannie Schanfield's home for a Hadassah (Jewish women's club) meeting. Rose spotted Fannie's "chiffon cake" on the table and lamented, "You, too, make those fluffy cakes! Why don't you make heavier ones?" Rose said that she preferred her mother's round cast-iron tube pan that baked a cake with real substance. Determined to have more of the Old World pans, the two friends decided to approach David Dalquist, founder of the Nordic Ware Company, which was just up the road from Rose's husband's business. When the women met Dalquist, he studied Rose's heavy pan and suggested they leave it with him so that he might consider creating something similar. In 1950, Nordic Ware began manufacturing and selling its Bundt pans. By the mid-1960s it had become the best-selling cake pan in America.

As an American classic, the Bundt is celebrated even in the movies. One of my favorite movie scenes is from *My Big Fat Greek Wedding.* When the groom's straitlaced, midwestern parents first visit the bride's boisterous Greek family bearing a Bundt cake, the Greek mother-in-law asks, "What is it?"

"A Bundt," replies the groom's mother.

"A *Bunk?*"

"No, a Bundt." This exchange continues for some time, concluding with the Greek mama's whispered inquiry to another family member, "Why is there a hole in it?"

Today, the all-American Bundt pan is owned by more than 60 million people *globally.* A friend of mine visited a small inn in Turkey where the proprietor served her—what else—a Bundt! When Rose Joshua, with the help of her son, informed Nordic Ware in 2005 that the company had not returned her pan, Rose, who lived in Jerusalem, received not only her pan (I am impressed the company still had it!) but dozens of other Bundt pans in a variety of sizes and shapes. Bundt pan, welcome to Israel!

Whether in German days of old, in a Minnesota kitchen or a Turkish inn, or on an Israeli kibbutz, the Bundt pan is still a dessert to be shared, to bring people together in the "bund" sense of the word. So, let's roll up our sleeves, put on our aprons, and get started!

Ingredients, Tools, and Preparation Tips

The beauty of the Bundt cake is that most often it can be made with little fuss from items found in your pantry. Nevertheless, a little information about ingredients will help you make a better Bundt.

COCOA

Recipes that call simply for "cocoa powder" refer to the familiar unsweetened, nonalkalyzed American baking cocoa, which is somewhat light in color. It may be called "natural." Another cocoa product, referred to in the recipes as "Dutch-process cocoa," has been alkalized, making it darker, slightly less acidic, and milder in flavor. Because the more acidic American version needs an alkaline ingredient like baking soda to bring out its flavor, the two cocoas should not be used interchangeably.

FLOUR

Flour comes in many varieties, but the four basic types are bread, cake, all-purpose, and self-rising. Bread flour is higher in gluten and will produce delicious bread, but heavy cakes. Cake flour, which has lower gluten content, makes light cakes but is more expensive and usually makes little noticeable difference in the final product. All-purpose flour—bleached or unbleached—works well for cakes, breads, and cookies. I prefer the unbleached, since the whitening agents add unnecessary chemicals to the flour. Self-rising flour, which contains salt and leaveners, is not suitable for most cakes. I kitchen-tested all the recipes in this book using all-purpose flour and switched to cake flour only when the results were significantly better. I have noted in these recipes where the use of cake flour makes a difference.

BUTTER

I know cooks who shudder in disgust at the notion of baking with regular salted butter. They strongly believe that only unsalted butter should be used for making cakes, breads, and cookies. These cooks use two basic arguments to support their stand: unsalted butter has a shorter shelf life and will therefore be fresher when it is sold, and salted butter adds unnecessary sodium to the finished product. Although I also tend to use unsalted butter for baking, I buy both, and I'll use whichever I have on hand. While kitchen-testing the recipes for this book, I used both kinds of butter and found little to no difference in the Bundts. So, I list the ingredient as butter and leave it up to you whether you want to use salted or unsalted.

EGGS

I tested these recipes using standard large Grade A eggs. I like to use eggs at room temperature because they blend more completely into the mixture. Given concerns about salmonella, however, I advise placing them in hot water for about five minutes to bring to room temperature.

EXTRACTS

While real, rather than artificial, extracts are expensive, they are worth it. Most artificial flavors have a great aroma, but their flavor bakes out, and you are left with a cake that falls short of your expectations. Buying extracts, particularly vanilla, in bulk is one way to save money. Or look for them in ethnic grocery stores; I have found wonderful vanilla at Mexican tiendas. Although vanilla is the most popular extract in American cooking, do not neglect lemon, orange, and almond extracts to boost the flavor of cakes, cookies, and breads.

TOOLS

Most cooking should be feasible without fancy, expensive equipment that has only a single function! However, there are a few tools that simply make cooking easier and the final product better. Here are a few essentials to making good Bundt cakes.

BUNDT PANS

Bundt pans come in three sizes: the standard 12-cup Bundt, the 9-cup Bundt, and the Mini-Bundt. The recipes in this book have been developed and tested for the 12-cup pan. The same batter can also be used with the other sized pans: For the 9-cup pan, use ⅔ of the batter and make the rest into cupcakes. The 12-cup quantity of batter will fill 12 Mini-Bundt forms.

A standard 12-cup Bundt will serve 10 to 12 generously. A 9-cup pan will provide 8 ample servings. The Mini-Bundt pans make 6 individual servings, which usually means baking a standard recipe in 2 batches.

FINE-MESH SIEVE

I remember seeing Bundt cakes at church potlucks when I was a kid, and they frequently had clumps of confectioners' sugar unevenly scattered over their sculpted tops. I used to wonder why and how that happened. Now I know; the bakers used a spoon to sprinkle sugar on top of the cake. This does not work. Other cakes were buried under a half an inch of confectioners' sugar. "Where is the cake?" I wondered. This baker tried to use a flour sifter to dust a Bundt and now knows better. Don't wreck your beautiful cake with imperfect powdering! For an even and fine layer of confectioners' sugar on your beautiful Bundt, invest in an inexpensive fine-mesh sieve. I guarantee you will be happy with the results.

PASTRY BRUSH

Bundt cakes may be "frosted" or finished in a variety of ways. One way is to spread a thin glaze over the top and sides of the cake. I will be honest; I have tried to do this with everything from a spatula to my fingers! None of those tools work. Invest in a good quality pastry brush, one with soft bristles that are firmly attached so that they don't fall out onto your cake.

Another piece of advice: use your pastry brush only for baked goods, not for marinades and BBQ sauces on the grill. Garlic, onion, and chilies will leave residues in the brush and impart odd tastes on your Bundt. After a Bundt has been glazed using a brush, I like to spoon additional glaze over the cake. This creates a lovely appearance.

SMALL STAINLESS-STEEL BOWL

Although many people use a double boiler for melting chocolate or making lemon curd, I have always used a stainless-steel bowl. It works fine and does not take up the space in my kitchen that a double boiler would. Place the bowl over a simmering pan of hot water, making sure that the bottom of the bowl does not touch the water. This is essential, since contact with the water will cause the chocolate to scorch.

MICRO-PLANE PEELER

If you have never used one of these creations, you are in for a real treat. Gone are the days of scraping your knuckles on a grater or having pieces of peel that are so large that they interrupt the flavor instead of enhancing it. This rather inexpensive tool produces perfect zest. Invest in one, and you will not be disappointed.

PREPARING THE PAN

The most common difficulty experienced while making Bundts is that they sometimes stick to the ornate pan forms. This can be avoided by properly preparing the pan. There are two basic approaches: grease and then flour the pan using a paper towel or your fingers, or use a oil-and-flour baking spray such as Baker's Joy. In my experience, both methods work very well, but Baker's Joy is especially helpful for intricate Bundts like the Cathedral, Rose, or Castle.

Three additional tips will help your Bundt come out of the pan intact:

- Do not overcook or undercook the cake.
- Allow the cake to cool *no more* than 15 minutes in the pan.
- Gently loosen the edges and the middle with a knife *before* inverting it.

TROUBLESHOOTING

We have all had baking or cooking projects that have gone awry. The stew so spicy your family could not eat it. The bread that is hard on top but doughy in the center. Fudge that is just a bit grainy. These things happen. The important trick is to know strategies to remedy any mishaps.

A FALLEN CAKE

My Bundt cake has fallen in the center! Should I throw it out? No, no, no! The beauty of the Bundt is that the part that could potentially fall ends up on the bottom.

In most cases it will not even be noticed when you flip the cake. If it has fallen, invert it onto a serving platter while it is warm, and the cake will settle evenly.

A BUNDT THAT STICKS

Factors such as humidity and uneven oven temperature can occasionally thwart even your best efforts to prevent sticking. But a partially stuck Bundt cake can be rescued.

- If only one small area is affected, simply serve the cake on individual plates that you prepare in the kitchen. Although it is attention-getting to be able to display an attractive whole Bundt cake to your dinner guests, this solution beats starting over.

- If just the top portion of the Bundt sticks, it may be possible to gently remove it, reposition it on the cake, and patch with a glaze. If your patching is visible, opt for a thicker frosting or whipped cream.

- If the damage is huge, not just the top or one small area, and your attempts at patching it remind you of Red Cross training, take a deep breath and let the cake cool. Slice it into small slabs and decoratively place it over sorbet or ice cream. If the flavors are compatible, make a batch of lemon curd. Fold in one cup of whipped cream, and then wedge the cake slices into this lemon mousse. I did this for an important work associate who adored the "fancy dessert." If the cake refuses to cut into even slabs, cube it and fold it into whipped cream that has been dressed up for the occasion with ginger, maple syrup, or some other accoutrement.

- If the cake has fallen in on itself, there may have been a rapid and large drop in barometric pressure. I saw it happen once. My Lemon Bundt looked like two layer cakes stacked on each other without benefit of filling or frosting. I needed the cake for a catering event and did not have time to make another one. What to do? Carefully, I separated the "layers" with a serrated knife. I whipped some heavy cream and folded in ½ cup sour cream to give it some tang; then folded in 1 cup of fresh blueberries. I placed this crème fraîche–whipped cream concoction between the layers and scattered lovely blueberries around the platter. It looked great, and my client said that cake was her favorite!

Enough instruction! This book is about doing, not reading. About you and your kitchen, not fussy rules or lots of fancy equipment.

Grab the Bundt pan and let the fun begin.

Chocolate Cakes

Chocolate Mayonnaise Cake

Mexican Hot Chocolate Mini-Bundt Cakes

Express Chocolate Espresso Bundt

Chocolate Cherry Fudge Bundt

Black and White Pound Cake

Chocolate and Peanut-Butter Chip Bundt

Chocolate Pound Cake

Low-Fat Chocolate Bundt

German Chocolate Bundt

Quick German Chocolate Bundt

Tunnel of Fudge Cake

Red Devil Cake

Chocolate Mayonnaise Cake

Despite this recipe's strange name and ingredient, I *love* this cake. Close your eyes. Imagine a birthday celebration in 1955. Picture a June Cleaver-esque mom with adoring eyes focused only on you. Now envision the moist chocolate cake of your dreams. This is that cake, and it is slathered in chocolate buttercream.

I bake this cake for my children in order to have something to say in my defense when, down the road, we inevitably enter therapy together. Bake this one and feel the love, but don't tell your children or guests about the mayonnaise until after they've eaten!

SERVES 10 TO 12

⅓ cup cocoa powder (make this a generous ⅓ cup)

1 cup boiling water

1½ teaspoons vanilla extract

¾ cup mayonnaise

2 cups sifted cake flour

2 teaspoons baking soda

1 cup sugar

½ teaspoon salt

> "I HAVE GONE TO FIVE WEDDINGS RECENTLY FOR WHICH THE BRIDE AND GROOM HAVE REGISTERED FOR BUNDT PANS AS GIFTS."
> BONNY WOLF, *TALKING WITH MY MOUTH FULL* (2006)

Preheat oven to 350°F. Prepare a 12-cup Bundt pan using butter and flour or Baker's Joy and set aside.

Whisk together cocoa and boiling water until smooth. Allow the mixture to cool to room temperature and whisk in vanilla and mayonnaise. (Your kids will want to taste the batter at this point—if you are mad at them, let them do it.) Combine the flour, baking soda, sugar, and salt. Mix on low speed for about 45 seconds. Add the chocolate mixture and beat for at least 1 minute.

Pour the batter into the prepared pans.

Bake for 25 to 30 minutes or until a toothpick comes out of the cake clean. Allow the cake to cool in the pan for 10 minutes and invert to a rack to finish cooling.

This cake is delicious with a variety of glazes, toppings, or frostings. It is most festive with a chocolate buttercream (page 133) or chocolate glaze (page 124). It is also good with a dusting of confectioners' sugar, a dollop of whipped cream, or a scoop of good-quality ice cream.

 GO WITH THE FLOW!

This is a forgiving and adaptable recipe. If you are out of vanilla, use brandy or whiskey. Although I prefer this cake made with cake flour, all-purpose flour will do in a pinch. The only hard and fast rule is do not substitute Miracle Whip for the mayonnaise—that sandwich-spread concoction is no miracle.

Mexican Hot Chocolate Mini-Bundt Cakes

This recipe is from Kim, one of my dearest and longtime friends. She also happens to be an outstanding baker. When we were 13 and 15, we used to pore over recipe books and cook together. In fact, the most memorable part of prom night was the five-course meal we slaved over for three days.

These Mini-Bundt cakes are delicious and very sensual. Crispy exterior, tender crumb, spicy hot and cinnamony. Kim recommends using Callebaut chocolate from Belgium, but any high-quality chocolate will work here. This cake is excellent with a glass of milk or a bowl of whipped cream. It would also make a stunning conclusion to an elegant dinner party or a late-night snack with someone very special. Although most 9-cup or 12-cup Bundt recipes can be used in Mini-Bundt pans, this recipe will *not* work in reverse in the larger pan.

A single Mini-Bundt form or cavity holds 1 cup of batter, compared to the standard 12-cup Bundt. Therefore, this recipe will make about 12 Mini-Bundts.

SERVES 12

2 cups flour

2 cups sugar, divided

1 teaspoon baking soda

½ teaspoon salt

¼ teaspoon cayenne pepper

1 to 2 tablespoons cinnamon

3 small eggs

½ cup buttermilk

1 cup butter

6 ounces bittersweet chocolate

½ cup cocoa powder

¾ cup espresso or strongly brewed coffee

2 tablespoons vanilla extract

¼ teaspoon almond extract

Preheat oven to 350°F. Grease and flour 12 Mini-Bundt forms and set aside. If you only have a Mini-Bundt pan with six cavities, bake this recipe in two batches.

Whisk together the flour, 1 cup of sugar, baking soda, salt, cayenne, and cinnamon in a large mixing bowl and set aside. Beat eggs and buttermilk together and set aside. Melt butter and chocolate together in the top of a double boiler or in a metal bowl suspended over hot water. Make sure that the bottom of the bowl does not touch the water. Add cocoa powder and espresso and stir until thoroughly combined. Add the egg mixture to the chocolate mixture.

Stir in the remaining 1 cup sugar, vanilla, and almond extract. Stir the wet ingredients into the dry ingredients. Mix until thoroughly combined and any lumps are dissolved. Pour the batter into the prepared Mini-Bundt pans.

Bake for 20 minutes exactly. Allow the Mini-Bundts to cool for 10 minutes before inverting them onto a wire rack to finish cooling.

These Mini-Bundts are delicious served plain or with a dollop of whipped cream or chocolate whipped cream.

 ROMANCE IN THE KITCHEN

Truly, these little Bundts are very seductive. And why not? They are filled with cayenne, cinnamon, chocolate, and . . . vanilla. Don't forget, vanilla extract worked for Granny on the television show *The Beverly Hillbillies;* it was her signature scent for special dates!

Express Chocolate Espresso Bundt

Imagine that you *need* chocolate now! This cake can go from an idea in your head to a cake in the oven in less then 10 minutes. Okay, so it uses a prepared cake mix. No one has to know, and the point of the Bundt is not pretension, but pleasure and ease. I made 12 of these Bundts for a gathering of senior citizens a few years ago and was delighted to hear my eight-year-old say to an 85-year-old man, "Oh, my goodness! Who gave you such a small piece of cake? We better fix that right away!" As she hoisted a healthy slab onto his plate, I heard him say under his breath, "I love that girl!" So do I.

SERVES 10 TO 12

CAKE

1 box (18-ounce) devil's food cake mix

1 small box instant chocolate pudding mix

4 eggs

½ cup strongly brewed coffee

½ cup vegetable oil

1 cup plain yogurt or sour cream

¼ cup cocoa powder

2 teaspoons instant espresso powder

GLAZE

¾ cup confectioners' sugar

3 tablespoons strongly brewed coffee

2 teaspoons instant espresso powder

Preheat oven to 350°F. Prepare a 12-cup Bundt pan using butter and flour or Baker's Joy and set aside.

Place the cake mix and pudding mix in a bowl and mix for 30 seconds on a low speed. Add the remaining ingredients and mix at medium speed for 4 minutes. Pour the batter into the pan.

Bake for 50 to 60 minutes or until a toothpick comes out of the cake clean. Let cake cool in the pan for 10 minutes, then turn out onto a wire rack or serving platter to cool completely.

To prepare glaze, combine confectioners' sugar, coffee, and espresso powder in a small bowl and beat until smooth. If glaze is not pourable, add a bit more coffee. If it is too thin, add a little more confectioners' sugar. Brush or spoon the glaze over the cake while it is still warm.

This cake works best with the espresso glaze. You can also serve it with chocolate buttercream (page 133) or a simple dusting of confectioners' sugar.

"YOU DON'T HAVE TO BE A FANCY BAKER TO BAKE A FANCY CAKE." PILLSBURY TELEVISION COMMERCIAL, 1972

Chocolate Cherry Fudge Bundt

When I think about this cake, I can almost smell our church basement before a potluck. Fudgy and sweet, this cake is comfort food. I got the recipe from my former boss and friend, Pat, who told me that it came from the mother of a childhood friend who, despite raising *seven* children, made a family dessert every day! This is a great cake to make with your kids or to let older children tackle on their own because it is virtually foolproof. This recipe also finally finds a use for canned cherry pie filling, for I certainly cannot bear to make a pie out of it!

SERVES 10 TO 12

1 box (18-ounce) devil's food cake mix

¼ cup vegetable oil

3 eggs

½ cup water

1 small can cherry pie filling

1 cup chocolate chips

Preheat oven to 350°F. Prepare a 12-cup Bundt pan using butter and flour or Baker's Joy and set aside.

Mix the cake mix briefly to break up any clumps. Add the remaining ingredients and beat at medium speed for about 3 minutes. Pour into the prepared pan.

Bake for 45 to 50 minutes, or until a toothpick comes out of the cake clean. Allow the cake to cool in the pan for 10 minutes and then invert to a rack or serving plate to finish cooling.

This cake is versatile. It is delicious served with a scoop of high-quality vanilla ice cream. I also like to dress it up by filling it with whipped cream. To fill, when the cake is thoroughly cooled, slice it in half horizontally. A long serrated knife works well for this task. Whip up some whipping cream (see page 136) and spread it over the bottom half of the cake. Top with the remaining cake half.

For an over-the-top presentation, add dollops of whipped cream on the cake at the fluted intervals and adorn each cloud with a drained maraschino cherry. Do this just before serving or use stabilized whipped cream (see page 137) and refrigerate until you are ready to devour it.

 COOKING WITH KIDS

Some of my biggest joys and most hair-raising frustrations come from cooking with my kids. We all know it is sometimes easier to just do it ourselves, but cooking is more than simply putting food on the table. It can be meaningful time spent together passing on knowledge of family tradition, food science, and math! I get a lump in my throat when I am making the same cinnamon rolls for my children that my mom made for me. How do I know how to make these? She let me, or made me, help! I hope someday my grandchildren will enjoy the same cinnamon rolls that they helped make. This can only happen if I take the time to teach my kids today.

Black and White Pound Cake

The Bundt pan has made it into the Smithsonian National Museum of American History as an icon of comfort food. Well, make this cake and feel comforted! I received this recipe from Mia, a friend of a friend. It seems fitting that Bundt recipes have come to me from near and far, from close friends and people I barely know. After all, this is the cake that has been drawing people together for over fifty years. Mia says that this is her very best cake and that there are two secrets to its creation: use medium or large, but not jumbo, eggs; and use Dutch cocoa like Nestle or Hershey, not fancy expensive, bitter ones.

SERVES 10 TO 12

2½ cups sifted flour
1¼ teaspoon baking powder
½ teaspoon salt
1¼ cup butter, softened
2½ cups sugar
5 eggs
2 teaspoons vanilla extract
1 cup minus 2 tablespoons milk
¼ cup Dutch-process cocoa, sifted

Preheat oven to 325°F. Prepare a 12-cup Bundt pan using butter and flour or Baker's Joy and set aside.

Sift flour, baking powder, and salt together and set aside. Cream butter for a few seconds and gradually add sugar. Beat until light and fluffy. Beat in eggs one at a time, creaming well after each addition. Add vanilla and beat. Add the flour mixture to the butter mixture, alternating with the milk. Remove 2 cups of the cake batter and blend the cocoa into it. Alternate spooning the light and chocolate batters into the prepared Bundt pan.

Bake for 70 minutes or until a toothpick comes out of the cake clean. Cool in pan about 10 minutes. Invert cake on wire rack to cool thoroughly.

This cake really needs no adornment. When my two-year-old saw this cake come out of the pan, he exclaimed, "Wow! How do you do that?" The tradition of dusting confectioners' sugar over Bundts mutes the dramatic effect of the two-toned cake. If you want to avoid a dry-looking exterior, slather the warm cake with honey butter (page 126).

An elegant way to serve this cake is to cut slices and place each slice on a plate that has been drizzled with zigzags of chocolate glaze (page 124). Servings also look lovely with tiny scoops of high-quality chocolate ice cream or French vanilla ice cream.

 ## EMBELLISHING WITH WHITE CHOCOLATE

White chocolate provides an easy to way to dramatize your Bundt. Melt 1 cup of white chocolate chips in a heat-proof bowl over simmering water; stir occasionally. Remove from the heat and add 3 teaspoons vegetable oil. Place wax paper or parchment paper on a baking sheet. Using a teaspoon, draw dots, hearts, zigzags, or even letters on the paper with the white chocolate mixture. Place the pan in the refrigerator for 7 minutes. Remove, peel off the designs, and place them on a dark serving platter or on individual plates around the cake for a beautiful decorative touch. These embellishments keep well, so you can make them ahead and store in a cool place.

Chocolate and Peanut-Butter Chip Bundt

You can thank an intern at the beautiful Randall Davey Audubon Center in Santa Fe, New Mexico, for this inspiration. The staff there diligently tested my cakes while I worked on this book. (I believe that they have added a Weight Watchers membership to the employee-benefits package.) One intern particularly loved the Peanut Butter and Jelly Bundt (page 66) I created, and she asked if I would make one featuring her two favorite flavors: peanut butter and chocolate. It took me three cakes to get it right, but I think this is it. The cake's chocolate and peanut butter are balanced, and each bite offers a sampling of each. This is a very cozy "comfort" cake for a simple family supper.

SERVES 10 TO 12

1 box (18-ounce) devil's food cake mix

1 small box instant chocolate pudding mix

1 cup water

4 eggs

⅓ cup vegetable oil

1 cup peanut-butter chips

Preheat oven to 350°F. Prepare a 12-cup Bundt pan using butter and flour or Baker's Joy and set aside.

Stir together the cake and the pudding mixes. Add the water, eggs, and oil and beat on medium for 4 minutes. Gently stir in the peanut-butter chips. Pour batter into the prepared pan.

Bake for 40 to 45 minutes or until a toothpick comes out of the cake clean. Cool for 10 minutes and invert onto a wire rack or serving platter to cool completely.

Prepare the peanut butter frosting on page 136. When the cake is cool, slice it horizontally with a serrated knife. Aim a little higher than halfway up. Flip the top half onto a plate. Spread ⅓ of the frosting on the bottom half, place the top half back on the frosted bottom, and spread the remaining ⅔ of the frosting on top. Top with shavings of dark chocolate.

 SPECULATION

"I got to thinking about relationships and partial lobotomies. Two seemingly different ideas that might just be perfect together—like chocolate and peanut butter." —Sarah Jessica Parker, "Sex and the City"

Chocolate Pound Cake

This cake is everything you want a chocolate pound cake to be: dense, rich, and earthy. I like to serve it after a simple meal of soup, bread, and salad. I have a friend who will reach for her third piece, then look away and say, "It's not a pound cake. Pound cakes do not contain chocolate." If you are a purist, call it whatever you like, but make a cup of coffee and enjoy this Bundt.

SERVES 10 TO 12

2 cups all-purpose flour

¾ cup cocoa powder

½ teaspoon baking powder

1 teaspoon salt

1½ cups butter, softened

2½ cups white sugar

5 eggs

2 teaspoons vanilla extract

2 teaspoons instant coffee granules dissolved in ¼ cup hot water

1 cup buttermilk

Preheat oven to 325°F. Prepare a 12-cup Bundt pan using butter and flour or Baker's Joy and set aside.

Mix together the flour, cocoa, baking powder, and salt. Set aside. In a large bowl, cream together the butter and sugar until light and fluffy, at least 3 minutes. Beat in the eggs one at a time and stir in the vanilla. Beat in the flour mixture alternating with the dissolved coffee and buttermilk. Pour batter into prepared pan.

Bake for 60 to 70 minutes, or until a toothpick inserted into the center of the cake comes out clean. Let cool in pan for 15 minutes, then turn out onto a wire rack and cool completely.

STENCILING YOUR CAKE

This is a simple way to dress up your Bundt cake. Plastic stencils of stars, moons, flowers, animals, and every imaginable shape are available in most craft stores. Simply wait until your Bundt has cooled, lay the stencils on the surface of the cake, and lightly dust with confectioners' sugar. Wait about three minutes and carefully remove the stencils with tweezers. This is quick way to personalize a child's birthday cake using letter stencils. This will work on the ridges of the Bundt providing the letters are small.

Another beautiful variation is to dust the cake with a mixture of confectioners' sugar and cocoa, using three parts confectioners' sugar and one part cocoa. Or try stenciling a lightly colored, frosted Bundt using pure cocoa.

Low-Fat Chocolate Bundt

Low-fat *and* delicious. I dedicate this recipe to a friend's mother who said that her Bundt pan was shoved into the back of the cupboard when she started dieting. Now we know better. Everyone needs treats, and it is possible to make delicious low-fat desserts. We just need to limit portions and how often we splurge. Get out that Bundt pan, because the unique shape makes it to tough to cheat on the size of a slice!

I adapted this chocolaty recipe from an Internet recipe at TheLeanWizard.com. Even if you are not counting calories, try it for a pleasant surprise.

SERVES 10 TO 12

⅓ cup drained, unsweetened applesauce
    (from ⅔ cup undrained sauce)

1¾ cups all-purpose flour

¾ cup Dutch-process cocoa

1½ teaspoons baking soda

⅓ cup unsalted butter, softened

1½ cups granulated sugar

2 teaspoons vanilla extract

1 egg

1 egg white

1½ cups reduced-fat sour cream

Preheat oven to 350°F. Prepare a 12-cup Bundt pan using butter and flour or Baker's Joy and set aside.

Place the applesauce in a strainer and set aside to drain for 15 minutes. Combine the flour, cocoa, and baking soda and set aside. Beat the butter in a large mixing bowl until light and fluffy. Measure and add ⅓ cup of drained applesauce and beat for 3 minutes. Add the sugar and beat for 3 minutes. Add the vanilla extract and beat for 15 seconds. Add the egg and egg white, beating after each addition. Add the sour cream and mix at medium speed until combined. Add the flour mixture and mix at lowest speed until just moistened, about 30 seconds. Pour the batter into the prepared pan and smooth the surface.

Bake for 40 to 45 minutes or until a toothpick comes out of the cake clean. Allow the cake to cool in the pan for 10 minutes and invert to a rack or serving plate to finish cooling.

This cake requires nothing other then a dusting of confectioners' sugar.

 USING THE INTERNET

The Internet provides a great way for accomplished cooks, and bakers just learning their way around a kitchen, to swap recipes, baking information, and creative ideas. When my daughter informed me the night before Halloween that it was our turn to bring a classroom snack— and could it be something new and different—it was the Internet to the rescue. A quick search brought up several easy, impressive ideas.

When I have fallen into a baking rut, I run a search on a dish or even on just an ingredient. Within seconds I have hundreds of recipes at my fingertips. Many sites also provide reviews by ordinary cooks who have tried the recipes. The reviews are helpful, sometimes very entertaining, and a great way to become a better cook.

German Chocolate Bundt

It's hard to beat a good German Chocolate cake. The gooey coconut, pecans, and caramel make just the right complement to the subtly flavored chocolate base. When you make this Bundt, keep it in plain sight of the guests during dinner so they can pace themselves and save room for this finale.

This recipe is adapted from Marion Cunningham's reprinting of the *Fannie Farmer Cookbook*. My spouse, who lived in Germany several times, said, "I cannot imagine why this is called German Chocolate cake. I *never* had any dessert this good in Germany." In fact, this cake is completely American—the name comes from the sweet chocolate used in the recipe.

SERVES 10 TO 12

CAKE

4 ounces Baker's German's Sweet Chocolate

½ cup boiling water

2¼ cups flour

½ teaspoon salt

1 teaspoon baking soda

1 cup butter, softened

2 cups sugar

4 eggs, separated

1 teaspoon vanilla extract

1 cup buttermilk

FILLING

1 cup evaporated milk

1 cup sugar

2 egg yolks, slightly beaten

½ cup butter

1 teaspoon vanilla

1½ cups Baker's Angel Flake coconut (sweetened)

1 cup chopped pecans

"YOUTH AND BEAUTY ARE FLEETING, BUT THE ABILITY TO BAKE A GOOD CHOCOLATE CAKE LASTS FOREVER."
CHRIS BROWNE, *HAGAR* COMIC STRIP

Preheat even to 350°F. Prepare a 12-cup Bundt pan using butter and flour or Baker's Joy and set aside.

Melt the chocolate in the boiling water. Do this in a double boiler or in a small stainless-steel bowl set over a pan of simmering water. Stir the chocolate thoroughly into the water and set aside to cool. Combine the flour with the salt and baking soda and set aside. Cream the butter and the sugar until fluffy. Add egg yolks one at a time, beating well after each addition. Blend in vanilla and chocolate. Add the flour alternately with the buttermilk to the sugar mixture. Beat after each addition until smooth. In another bowl, beat the egg whites until stiff but not dry. Carefully fold them into the batter until the white streaks disappear. Pour the batter into the prepared pan.

Bake for 35 to 40 minutes or until a toothpick comes out of the cake clean. Do not be alarmed if the top has fallen slightly. Cool in the pan for 15 minutes and invert onto a wire rack or serving platter.

To prepare the frosting, mix the evaporated milk, sugar, egg yolks, butter, and vanilla in a saucepan and stir over medium heat until thickened. This should take between 10 and 15 minutes, depending on heat and humidity. Stir in the coconut and nuts. Cool until frosting is thick enough to spread. When the cake is cool, slice it horizontally with a serrated knife. Aim a little higher than halfway up. Flip the top half onto a plate. Spread ⅓ of the frosting on the bottom half and place the top half back on the frosted cake. Spread the remaining ⅔ of the frosting on top.

WEDDING BELLS!

You can use the Bundt theme to create a lovely wedding gift that will be used for decades. Simply place a Bundt pan, several hand-copied family recipes, and a serving platter in a rustic basket. You will be remembered year after year when the couple makes cakes for family dinners and special occasions.

Quick German Chocolate Bundt

Two recipes for German chocolate cake? Well, sometimes you are short on time and long on desire for this gooey creation. I developed this quick but very tasty version of the classic the day I was juggling my fretting two-year-old and a house guest who had a strong desire for German chocolate cake. The ten minutes it took to get this cake in the oven satisfied both! Enjoy!

SERVES 10 TO 12

CAKE

1 box (18-ounce) German chocolate
    cake mix

4 eggs

1 cup water

½ cup vegetable oil

½ cup sour cream

1 teaspoon vanilla extract

FILLING

1 cup evaporated milk

1 cup sugar

2 egg yolks, slightly beaten

½ cup butter

1 teaspoon vanilla

1½ cups Baker's Angel Flake
    coconut

1 cup chopped pecans

"PEOPLE WHO FEEL THEY MUST MAKE A REAL DESSERT ARE OFTEN LOOKING FOR SOMETHING SIMPLE AND WONDERFUL, TWO WORDS FELT TO BE MUTUALLY EXCLUSIVE. I LIKE A CAKE THAT TAKES ABOUT FOUR SECONDS TO PUT TOGETHER AND GIVES AN AMBROSIAL RESULT. FORTUNATELY, THERE ARE SUCH CAKES."

LAURIE COLWIN, *MORE HOME COOKING* (1993)

Preheat oven to 350°F. Prepare a 12-cup Bundt pan using butter and flour or Baker's Joy and set aside.

Beat together cake mix, water, eggs, oil, sour cream, and vanilla until very fluffy, about 4 minutes. Pour it into the prepared pan.

Bake for 50 to 55 minutes or until a toothpick comes out of the cake clean. Allow the cake to cool in the pan for 10 minutes and invert to a rack or serving plate to finish cooling.

To make the filling, mix the evaporated milk, sugar, egg yolks, butter, and vanilla in a saucepan and stir over medium heat until thickened. This should take between 10 and 15 minutes, depending on heat and humidity. Stir in the coconut and nuts. Cool until it is thick enough to spread.

When the cake is cool, slice it horizontally with a serrated knife. Aim a little higher than halfway up. Flip the top half onto a plate. Spread ⅓ of the frosting on the bottom half and place the top half back on the frosted cake. Spread the remaining frosting on top.

Tunnel of Fudge Cake

This is the probably the most famous Bundt cake ever made. It won a $5,000 prize in the 1966 Pillsbury Bakeoff and almost single handedly started the Bundt craze. If you Google the name today, you will be inundated with hundreds of very similar recipes. Every last one of them says in an ominous tone: "Do not omit the nuts—they are essential!" I never have, but I am very curious to know what might happen.

I adapted this recipe from one in my mother's collection. When the cake is baked and cut, your guests will be delighted to find a tunnel of fudge in each piece.

Don't use the toothpick method to test the cake. You will intersect the tunnel of fudge and keep the cake in oven too long. You will know the cake is done when it pulls away from the sides of the pan and it springs back when lightly touched.

SERVES 10 TO 12

CAKE

2¼ cups flour

¾ cup cocoa powder

1¾ cups sugar

1¾ cups butter, softened

6 eggs

2 cups confectioners' sugar

2 cups chopped walnuts or pecans

GLAZE

¾ cup confectioners' sugar

¼ cup cocoa powder

4 to 6 teaspoons of milk or half-and-half

Heat oven to 350°F. Prepare a 12-cup Bundt pan using butter and flour or Baker's Joy and set aside.

Combine flour and cocoa powder and set aside. In a large bowl, cream sugar and butter until light and fluffy. Add eggs one at a time, beating well after each addition. Gradually add 2 cups confectioners' sugar and mix until thoroughly incorporated. Stir in flour mixture by hand until well blended. Gently stir in the nuts. Spoon the rather thick batter into the prepared pan.

Bake for 45 to 50 minutes or until the top is set and edges are beginning to pull away from sides of pan. Cool upright *in pan* on wire rack for 1½ hours to allow the fudge to set. Invert onto serving plate to cool thoroughly.

To make the glaze, combine confectioners' sugar and cocoa powder with 4 tablespoons of milk or half-and-half. Mix thoroughly and add only enough milk to create a smooth, but pourable glaze. Spoon or brush the glaze over the top of the cake, allowing some to run down sides.

The classic recipe for Tunnel of Fudge calls for a chocolate glaze, which provides a double whammy of chocolate. Alternately, this cake is delicious with cocoa-scented whipped cream (page 137) or a scoop of high-quality vanilla ice cream or coffee ice cream.

 ## ALICE AND THE BRADY BUNCH

According to several experts and my own research, Alice (played by Ann B. Davis), who was cook and chief bottlewasher to television's Brady Bunch, the most famous blended family of the 1970s, never once made a Bundt cake for the six Brady children! I hope this was noted in her annual performance review.

Red Devil Cake

My 92-year-old grandmother has made this cake for birthday celebrations for her children, grandchildren, and great-grandchildren—approximately 150 times—and it is always a hit. A few years ago, she hand-copied our family recipes into a notebook for my birthday. I was thrilled, but surprised. Her recipes contain only lists of ingredients; no notes on method, baking, or finishing. When I asked her about that she said, "Well, I didn't know that you were an idiot!" Enough said.

The unusual red color of this cake adds to its charm. Bake it in a rose-form Bundt pan for Mother's Day. I have also made the cake at Halloween—I swore to the children that it is made with real blood. Some vanilla frosting drizzled with fake blood and a butcher knife add to the effect. Go for beauty or for gore—either way, enjoy this Bundt!

SERVES 10 TO 12

2 ounces red food coloring

4 heaping tablespoons cocoa powder

½ cup shortening

1½ cups sugar

2 eggs

1 cup buttermilk

½ teaspoon salt

1 teaspoon vanilla extract

2 cups flour

1 teaspoon vinegar

1 teaspoon baking soda

Preheat oven to 350°F. Prepare a 12-cup Bundt pan using butter and flour or Baker's Joy and set aside.

Combine cocoa and food coloring, and let mixture stand. Cream the shortening and sugar thoroughly. Add the eggs. Add the buttermilk, salt, vanilla, and flour and beat thoroughly. Beat in the vinegar and baking soda by hand. Pour the batter into the pan.

Bake for 45 to 50 minutes or until the cake springs back slightly when touched. Cool for 10 minutes in the pan before inverting it onto wire rack or serving platter to cool thoroughly.

My grandma always used butter vanilla frosting (page 132) for our cakes. If you are using a rose Bundt pan, use only a sprinkling of confectioners' sugar, and scatter rose petals on the serving platter.

 FAKE BLOOD FOR HALLOWEEN

This recipe makes real-looking blood, a wonderfully gory touch on the Red Devil Cake. For the best appearance use a light hand and practice caution because the mixture can stain.

Recipe: Combine ½ cup corn syrup, 1 teaspoon red food coloring, and two drops blue food coloring. Place in a glass container and shake vigorously. Voila!

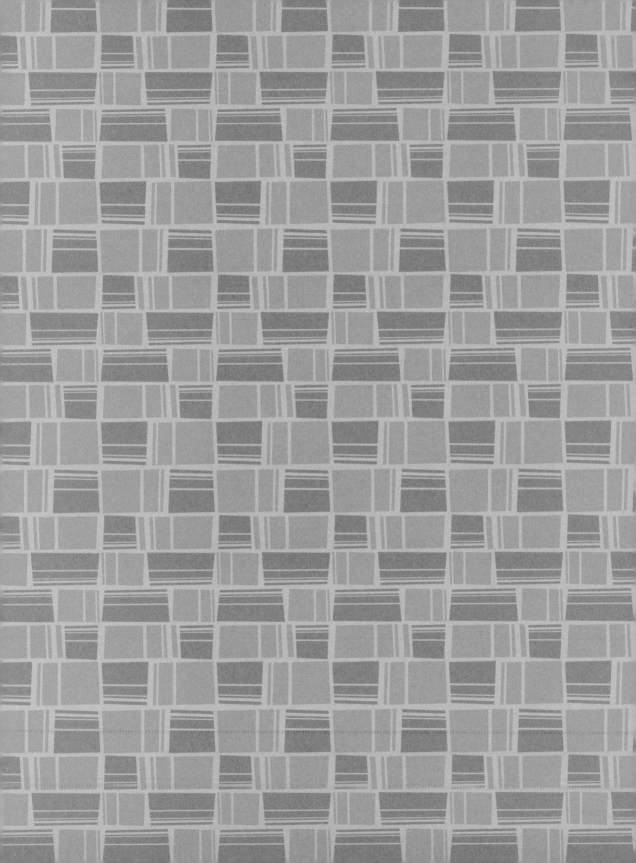

Coffee Cakes

Apricot Almond Pound Cake

Quick Lemon Poppy Seed Cake

Bubble Loaf

Sour Cream Coffee Cake

Rhubarb Pecan Cake

Cinnamon Swirl Coffee Cake

Maple Corn Coffee Cake

Sunday Pecan Coffee Cake

Sour Cream Walnut Streusel Coffee Cake

Glazed Almond Bundt Cake

Hungarian Cheese-Filled Coffee Cake

Apricot Almond Pound Cake

My spouse says this is the best Bundt in the book. I developed this cake for a winter brunch that needed a whisper of spring and a taste of fruit. Having tired of apples and citrus, I turned to apricot preserves for inspiration. I now serve this recipe year around, and although I often make it for breakfast or tea, I sometimes serve it to enthusiastic guests for a dinner dessert.

I once brought this cake to a toddler play date where a sugar-conscious mother assured me that *her* child really did not enjoy sweets. I kept my comments to myself as I watched her daughter eat three pieces!

SERVES 10 TO 12

CAKE

2½ cups flour

2 teaspoons baking powder

1 teaspoon baking soda

1 teaspoon salt

1 cup butter, softened

1 cup sugar

3 eggs

1 teaspoon almond extract

1 cup sour cream

½ cup apricot preserves

GLAZE

½ cup apricot preserves

Juice of half a lemon

½ cup water

Preheat oven to 350°F. Prepare a 12-cup Bundt pan using butter and flour or Baker's Joy and set aside.

Combine dry ingredients and set aside. Beat the butter for several seconds in a large mixing bowl. Add the sugar and beat until smooth. Add the eggs and almond extract and beat for 2 to 3 minutes or until light and fluffy. Add the flour mixture and beat until smooth. Add the sour cream and mix well. In a small bowl, whip ½ cup of the apricot preserves until light and the larger pieces of apricot have been broken into smaller bits. Pour half of the batter into the prepared pan. Spoon the preserves into the center taking care that the preserves don't touch the sides of the pan. Spoon the remaining batter on top, being sure to completely envelope the preserves.

Bake for 50 minutes or until a toothpick comes out of the cake clean. Let it cool in the pan for 10 minutes, and then turn onto a serving plate.

To prepare the glaze, combine in a small saucepan the remaining ¼ cup of apricot preserves, the lemon juice, and water. Bring to a boil and beat until combined and the larger apricot pieces of have broken into smaller bits. The glaze should be slightly thickened, but thin enough to pour. If it is too thick, add more water. If it is too thin, cook longer. Spoon or brush the glaze over the hot cake, taking care to cover it thoroughly.

This cake serves beautifully with fresh flowers strewn around the platter, particularly apricot-colored Gerbera daisies. I also like to serve this on a large platter with a variety of dried fruits placed decoratively around the edges.

Quick Lemon Poppy Seed Cake

Here is a Bundt that comes together in minutes and keeps well for several days—if family members don't nibble it away. The crunchy poppy seeds work nicely on the subtly flavored lemon background. I received this recipe from a busy mom who often uses it as an after-school snack or when she needs to provide treats for a large group of kids. It is firm enough to be eaten on the go without being overly heavy or dense.

Dads: This is a good recipe for your children to make for Mother's Day. Mom will like it, and the kids can feel that they have done something very special for Mom.

SERVES 10 TO 12

¼ cup poppy seeds

¼ cup milk

1 box (18-ounce) lemon cake mix

1 small box instant vanilla pudding mix

1 cup water

½ cup vegetable oil

4 eggs

½ cup sour cream or plain yogurt

"YOU GUYS LIKE A BAKE SALE, RIGHT? I MEAN WE NEED MONEY FOR THE DANCE RECITAL, AND YOU KNOW I DO AN EMPOWERING LEMON BUNDT!"
BUFFY THE VAMPIRE SLAYER (TELEVISION CHARACTER), SEASON 4

Preheat oven to 350°F. Prepare a 12-cup Bundt pan using butter and flour or Baker's Joy and set aside.

Soak poppy seeds in milk and set aside. Stir together cake mix and pudding mix in a large bowl, making sure to break up any clumps. Make a well in the center of the floury mixture and pour in water, oil, and eggs. Beat on low speed until blended. Scrape bowl, and beat 4 minutes on medium speed. Blend in poppy seed mixture and sour cream. Pour batter into the prepared pan.

Bake for 60 minutes, or until a toothpick inserted into the center of the cake comes out clean. Let cool in pan for 10 minutes, then turn out onto a wire rack or plate to cool completely.

This cake is wonderful with the Lemon Glaze (page 127). The sweet-and-tart glaze creates a pleasing contrast to the otherwise mellow flavor of the cake. You can also serve it with just a dusting of confectioners' sugar or a dollop of whipped cream.

 GO FOR THE DRAMATIC PRESENTATION

Don't be afraid to try something new when you are serving your Bundt cake. A grating of chocolate, slices of fresh fruit, or a splash of raspberry sauce turn a good dessert into a fantastic one.

Bubble Loaf

When my brother was born, my older sister's only response was, "Oh. Where is the bubble loaf?" Once you have tasted this you will know why it trumped the birth of my brother. This is recognizable as my mother's recipe through and through because it calls for butter in *three* places! I remember her making this during a snow-day blizzard. It is sweet and light and delightful.

SERVES 8

CAKE

⅔ cup sugar

1 teaspoon cinnamon

6 teaspoons yeast

1 teaspoon sugar

¾ cup warm water

2¼ cup milk, scalded

1 teaspoon salt

¾ cup sugar

¾ cup butter

3 eggs

8 cups flour

½ cup butter, melted

1 cup finely chopped pecans

GLAZE

½ cup sugar

1 cup chopped pecans

¼ cup melted butter

1 teaspoon cinnamon

¼ cup corn syrup

Preheat oven to 350°F. Generously butter a 12-cup Bundt pan and set aside.

Combine ⅔ cup sugar and 1 teaspoon cinnamon and set aside. Combine yeast with 1 teaspoon sugar and warm water, and set aside until it is foamy. Scald the milk. Add salt, ¾ cup sugar, and ¾ cup butter. Cool mixture to lukewarm, add yeast mixture, stir, and pour into a large bowl. Add the eggs one at a time, beating after each addition. Add flour one cup at a time, beating well after each cup. The dough will be quite sticky. Put dough in a greased bowl and let it rise in a warm place until double.

Flour a wooden board or counter and place the dough on it. Form dough into a 12-inch long roll and cut into 24 pieces. Form each piece into a ball, dip each piece in melted butter, roll in the cinnamon-sugar, and then roll in the nuts. Place balls in the prepared pan on top of each other and let dough rise for about 30 minutes.

Bake for 35 to 40 minutes. If the top begins to brown too much, cover with foil. Let cake cool for 10 minutes in the pan and invert on a serving platter.

To glaze the loaf, combine the sugar, nuts, butter, cinnamon, and corn syrup in a small saucepan and heat gently until the sugar is dissolved and the mixture is thoroughly combined. Pour the glaze over the inverted loaf and serve. Although it is delicious at room temperature, it really shines when you serve it warm.

"COOKING IS ONE OF THE LEGACIES WE CAN LEAVE TO THE FUTURE, AND I WOULD LIKE TO BE REMEMBERED FOR MY BAKING. WE ALL KNOW WE ARE NOT IMMORTAL, BUT AFTER I AM GONE, I WOULD LIKE MY SON AND DAUGHTER TO BE ABLE TO SAY, 'OUR MOTHER MADE REAL YEAST BREAD FOR BREAKFAST.'"

MARION CUNNINGHAM, *THE BREAKFAST BOOK*

Sour Cream Coffee Cake

I got this recipe from my mother-in-law. She is a first-class baker, and I am not just saying this because she might read this book. Over the years, I would guess, she has made dozens of these sour cream dreams for church events. The cake can be made the night before you need it without becoming the least bit dry. It is rich without being cloying, and it can stand alone or hold its own with lemon curd, fresh fruit, or even a caramel sauce. For an old-fashioned taste try it with the old-fashioned lemon sauce (page 142).

SERVES 10 TO 12

3 cups cake flour

¼ teaspoon baking powder

3 cups sugar

1 cup butter

6 eggs, separated

1 cup sour cream

1 teaspoon vanilla extract

1 teaspoon almond extract

1 teaspoon lemon extract

Preheat oven to 325°F. Prepare a 12-cup Bundt pan using butter and flour or Baker's Joy and set aside.

Combine flour and baking powder and set aside. Beat egg whites until stiff but not dry and set aside. Beat the sugar and butter until fluffy. Add egg yolks one at a time, combining thoroughly after each addition. Add flour mixture and flavorings, and mix until incorporated. Gently but thoroughly fold in the egg whites until no white streaks appear in the batter. Pour into the prepared pan.

Bake for 1 hour and 15 minutes, or until a toothpick comes out of the cake clean. Let cool in pan for 10 minutes, then turn out onto a wire rack to cool completely.

This is an incredibly adaptable cake. It is delicious served with just a dusting of confectioners' sugar. For a change of pace, serve it with raspberry rhubarb sauce (page 142) from a bowl or drizzled on each plate. The cake also makes a lovely brunch cake presented with a bowl of fresh strawberries or chilled lemon curd (page 141). I once pleased some unexpected guests with slabs of this cake drizzled with butterscotch sauce (page 140).

 ## CUTTING THE CAKE

I learned this trick on a camping trip in Norway years ago. One of the teenage participants was having a birthday, so the leader tucked a pound cake in his back-pack. When it came time to slice it, no one had a suitable clean knife for the task. An enterprising camper leapt to her feet and returned with some dental floss. With eight deft movements, she created 16 perfect wedges of cake. Remember this trick for emergencies or for especially dense cakes. It works like a charm.

Rhubarb Pecan Cake

I love rhubarb. It is classic Minnesota. I can never seem to grow enough of it myself, but whenever I am tempted to pay $2.99 a pound at the grocery store, I hear my grandmother's voice saying, "You paid *what* for pie plant?"

While I love rhubarb pie, I cherish this recipe for rhubarb coffee cake, developed by combining several basic coffee cake recipes. When my daughter was younger, she could never remember the word rhubarb and repeatedly asked for barbeque cake.

SERVES 10 TO 12

2¼ cups flour

1 teaspoon baking soda

½ teaspoon salt

1 teaspoon cinnamon

½ teaspoon cardamom

1 cup plus 3 teaspoons sugar

¾ cup brown sugar

½ cup butter, softened

1 egg

1 cup buttermilk

1½ teaspoons vanilla extract

2 cups rhubarb, chopped

1 cup walnuts or pecans

Preheat the oven to 350°F. Prepare a 12-cup Bundt pan using butter and flour or Baker's Joy and set aside.

Combine flour, baking soda, and salt and set aside. Combine cinnamon, cardamom, and 3 teaspoons of sugar and set aside. Beat remaining white sugar, brown sugar, and butter until fluffy and beat in the egg. Add flour mixture and blend thoroughly. Add buttermilk and vanilla and mix just until blended. Stir in the rhubarb and the nuts. Place half of the batter in the pan and smooth out the surface. Sprinkle it with half of the sugar mixture. Pour the remaining batter in the pan and sprinkle with the remaining sugar and spices.

Bake for 45 to 50 minutes, or until a toothpick comes out of the cake clean. Let cake cool in pan for 10 minutes, then turn out onto a wire rack to cool completely.

This cake needs only a light dusting of confectioners' sugar. If you want to gussy it up a bit, serve it with some freshly whipped cream scented with ginger (page 137).

"NO ONE WHO COOKS, COOKS ALONE. EVEN AT HER MOST SOLITARY, A COOK IN THE KITCHEN IS SURROUNDED BY GENERATIONS OF COOKS PAST, THE ADVICE AND MENUS OF COOKS PRESENT, THE WISDOM OF COOKBOOK WRITERS." LAURIE COLWIN, FOOD WRITER

Cinnamon Swirl Coffee Cake

One of the best things about this coffee cake is the aroma that it dispatches throughout your house when it is baking in the oven. Growing up in Michigan during the 1970s, my siblings and I had our fair share of stay-at-home "snow days." At the mere prospect of a snow day, my father would call home from church (he was a minister) and tell my teenage brother and me to call all our friends to spend the night! Sometimes my father was wrong, and we would all bitterly drag ourselves to school the next day. But what a time we had when he was right! My mother would make a huge breakfast: bacon, eggs, toast, coffee and this cinnamon coffee cake. The aroma would drive us from our beds. This is a dressed-down, informal version of the Sour Cream Walnut Streusel Coffee Cake on page 52.

SERVES 10 TO 12

2½ cups flour

1 teaspoon baking soda

1 teaspoon baking powder

1¼ cups sugar, divided

½ cup brown sugar

3 eggs

¾ cup butter, softened

1 cup sour cream or low-fat yogurt

1½ teaspoons vanilla extract

¾ cup chopped nuts

2½ teaspoons cinnamon

Preheat oven to 375°F. Prepare a 12-cup Bundt pan using butter and flour or Baker's Joy and set aside.

Combine dry ingredients and set aside. Beat 1 cup sugar, ½ cup brown sugar, and eggs until light and fluffy. Add the butter and sour cream and beat well. Add the flour mixture and combine thoroughly. Stir in vanilla and nuts.

Mix the remaining ¼ cup of sugar and cinnamon and set aside.

Put half of the batter in the pan, sprinkle with the cinnamon mixture, and top with the remaining batter.

Bake for 45 to 50 minutes or until a toothpick comes out of the cake clean. Let cool in pan for 10 minutes, then turn out onto a wire rack or serving platter to cool.

Serve warm with a strong cup of coffee. It requires absolutely no adornment.

 "BUNDT CAKE, BUNDT PAN" BY DAVID FRANKS

The Bundt cake is turned out to cool
From the Bundt pan, a specialized tool
For the baker. It's fluted—
A ring, convoluted.
Nice pan, and the cake makes me drool.

Maple Corn Coffee Cake

This coffeecake shouts Thanksgiving morning. It is moist and dense with the undertones of corn, walnuts, and pure maple syrup. Although it is superb when served warm, it keeps well overnight. This would be the perfect coffee cake to nibble on while you stuff the bird or to serve to guests who are helping prepare the feast.

While many cakes echo tastes and traditions from other places, this one is all-American. I adapted it from a recipe out of *Blue Corn and Chocolate* by Elisabeth Rozin, a delightful book that celebrates New World foods. The addition of little maple sugar candies on each individual plate makes this easy-to-make cake feel very special.

SERVES 10 TO 12

CAKE

1 ear of fresh sweet corn or
    ½ cup canned whole
    kernel corn

1 tablespoon butter, if using
    fresh corn

½ cup butter, softened

1 cup sugar

3 eggs

1½ teaspoons vanilla extract

1 teaspoon bourbon

1⅜ cups flour

1½ teaspoons baking soda

½ teaspoon salt

½ cup cornmeal

⅔ cup buttermilk

1 cup chopped walnuts (black
    walnuts are especially delicious)

MAPLE GLAZE

⅓ cup pure maple syrup

Preheat the oven to 350°F. Prepare a 12-cup Bundt pan using butter and flour or Baker's Joy and set aside.

Remove the corn from the cob and gently sauté in 1 tablespoon butter until lightly cooked, about 3 minutes, and set it aside. (If you are using canned corn, drain the ½ cup and set aside.) In a large bowl, beat the butter and sugar together until light and fluffy. Add the eggs one at a time, beating after each addition. Add the vanilla and bourbon and mix thoroughly. In a third bowl, combine the flour, baking soda, salt, and cormeal and set aside. Add this mixture, alternating with the buttermilk, to the butter-sugar mixture, mixing well after each addition. Stir in the corn and chopped walnuts. Pour the batter into the prepared pan.

Bake for 45 to 50 minutes or until a toothpick comes out of the cake clean. Allow the cake to cool for 10 minutes before inverting it onto either a baking sheet or a serving platter that is oven-safe.

For the glaze, gently heat the maple syrup in the microwave until hot, about 20 seconds. Watch this carefully, as microwave temperatures vary and syrup can easily boil over. Brush the syrup over the cake allowing it to soak in before adding more. The cake should be completely covered so that no "dry" areas remain on it. Place the cake back into the oven for 5 minutes. Although you will have turned off the heat, enough warmth will remain to melt the syrup into the cake. Remove and cool. This earthy cake does not even need confectioners' sugar before serving.

"SEX IS GOOD, BUT NOT AS GOOD AS FRESH SWEET CORN." GARRISON KEILLOR, HUMORIST

Sunday Pecan Coffee Cake

A low-fat coffee cake that really packs a punch! It balances sweet and savory, and rich dairy with crunchy nuttiness. A similar cake is served at the Wickwood Country Inn in Saugatuck, Michigan. Sophisticated enough to be served at a formal brunch, it is also easy to make. You can pull it together for family on a lazy Saturday. (My dad is a minister, so I was never allowed lazy Sundays.)

SERVES 10 TO 12

FILLING

½ cup chopped pecans, toasted

¼ cup brown sugar

1⅛ teaspoons cinnamon

CAKE

2 cups flour

½ teaspoon salt

1 teaspoon baking powder

½ cup non-fat plain yogurt

½ cup low-fat cottage cheese

2 cups sugar

¼ cup canola oil

1 tablespoon minced lemon zest

1 egg

2 egg whites

2 teaspoons lemon juice

2⅛ teaspoons vanilla extract

Preheat the oven to 350°F. Prepare a 12-cup Bundt pan using butter and flour or Baker's Joy and set aside.

Combine the pecans, brown sugar, and cinnamon for the filling and set aside. Combine flour, salt, and baking powder and set aside. In a blender or food processor, combine yogurt and cottage cheese and set aside. Beat sugar, oil, and lemon zest thoroughly. Mix in egg and egg whites.

Add the yogurt mixture to the egg mixture. Add the lemon juice and vanilla.

Stir the flour mixture into the egg mixture just until combined. Do not over mix.

Pour ⅔ of the batter into the prepared pan. Sprinkle the filling evenly into the pan. Top with remaining batter.

Bake for 40 to 45 minutes or until a toothpick comes out of the cake clean. Cool for 10 minutes and invert on a serving plate.

This coffee cake does not require further adornment, but a simple dusting of confectioners' sugar or a few fresh berries strewn on the plate finish it nicely.

 ## THE IMPORTANCE OF TOASTING NUTS

I love nuts! They add depth and texture to almost any baked delicacy. But in order to get the most flavor out of nuts, they need to be toasted. Place them in a metal baking pan in a 350° oven for about 5 minutes. Watch them carefully—they burn quite quickly. You will love the aroma that wafts through your kitchen, as well as the way they enhance and make your cakes taste richer.

Sour Cream Walnut Streusel Coffee Cake

I received this recipe from a friend of a friend, who tells a very charming story about this Bundt. When she was in college her parents would visit and take her out to eat, hoping to put a little meat on her bones. They always ended up at a small café that had the best wine selection and incredible desserts. Several years later one of the café's recipes showed up in the restaurant section of *Bon Appetit*. She and her mom were so excited! It was one of their favorites, a sour cream and streusel coffee cake. Although they wouldn't be together for Christmas, they decided to both make it and exchange pictures in a contest. The daughter decorated it with a fancy garland and used confectioners' sugar on top instead of icing. Her mother, going for the emotional vote, took a picture of her gorgeous creation cake with the younger sister holding it. Naturally, they both won, and they made it a staple for every Christmas morning. Once you taste it, you will too.

SERVES 10 TO 12

CAKE

1¼ cups coarsely chopped walnuts

1¼ cups (packed) golden brown sugar

4½ teaspoons ground cinnamon

4½ teaspoons unsweetened cocoa powder

6 tablespoons dried currants

3 cups cake flour

1½ teaspoons baking soda

1½ teaspoons baking powder

1 teaspoon salt

¾ cup butter, room temperature

1½ cups sugar

3 large eggs

1 tablespoon vanilla extract

16 ounces sour cream

SUGAR GLAZE

1 cup confectioners' sugar

1 tablespoon milk

Preheat oven to 350°F. Prepare a 12-cup Bundt pan using butter and flour or Baker's Joy and set aside.

Mix first 5 ingredients in a small bowl and set aside. Sift flour, baking soda, baking powder and salt into medium bowl and set aside. Beat the butter and 1½ cups sugar in large bowl until blended. Beat in eggs 1 at a time. Mix in vanilla. Add dry ingredients and sour cream alternately into butter mixture in 3 additions. Beat batter on high 1 minute. Scrape ⅓ of the batter into the prepared pan. Sprinkle with half of the nut mixture. Spoon ⅓ of batter over it. Sprinkle with remaining nut mixture. Spoon the remaining batter over it.

Bake 1 hour or until a toothpick comes out of the cake clean. Cool cake in pan on rack for 10 minutes and invert to wire rack or serving platter.

To make the glaze, whisk confectioners' sugar and milk in small bowl until smooth. Drizzle the glaze over the warm cake. Although it is best served warm, it is also delicious at room temperature.

"BUTTER VS. MARGARINE? I TRUST COWS OVER SCIENTISTS." UNKNOWN

Glazed Almond Bundt Cake

I found this recipe on Allrecipes.com, donated by Judy Patterson. I was looking for something with intense almond flavor that did not involve almond paste, and with a few minor changes to Judy's creation, I developed this. Rich and comforting, it makes a brunch or Sunday morning feel special. Thank you, Judy!

SERVES 10 TO 12

CAKE

2½ cups flour

2 teaspoons baking powder

½ teaspoon salt

½ cup ground almonds

1 cup butter, softened

1½ cups sugar

4 eggs

1½ teaspoons almond extract

2 teaspoons vanilla extract

1 cup milk

ALMOND GLAZE

¼ cup milk

¾ cup sugar

½ teaspoon almond extract

½ cup toasted sliced almonds

Preheat oven to 350°F. Prepare a 12-cup Bundt pan using butter and flour or Baker's Joy and set aside.

Mix together flour, baking powder, salt, and ground almonds and set aside. In a large bowl, beat butter with 1½ cups sugar until light and fluffy. Beat in the eggs one at a time, beating well after each addition. Stir in the almond and vanilla extracts. Stir in the flour mixture alternating with the milk, mixing only until blended. Pour it into the prepared pan.

Bake for 60 to 70 minutes or until a toothpick comes out of the cake clean. Let it cool in the pan for 10 minutes, then turn out onto a wire rack. Cool 10 minutes longer. Place the rack over wax paper to catch the topping drips.

To make the topping, place all of the ingredients in a saucepan and bring to a boil. Reduce the heat and stir until sugar is dissolved and the mixture is slightly thickened. Pour the topping over the warm cake and serve warm or at room temperature.

 HOW TO GRIND ALMONDS

Ground almonds are a great addition to many cakes and tarts, but if you simply throw them into your food processor and press the On button, they can easily turn into a gummy mess. To avoid this, add about 1 tablespoon of sugar per cup of almonds and gently pulse. This will produce finely ground almonds and make cleaning your food processor a snap.

Hungarian Cheese-Filled Coffee Cake

This is a keeper! I got this recipe from Anne Kaplan, a friend and colleague at the Minnesota Historical Society. Her family tradition was to drizzle some apricot preserves over the cooling cake and then lightly dust it with confectioners' sugar. She explains that a schism occurred in the family over whether this last step should be omitted for health reasons. I tried it both ways, and I say keep it in! Let's be honest, this cake has cream cheese, butter, and sour cream in it. Leaving out confectioners' sugar does not make it a dieter's dream. The tangy preserves and sugar perfectly balance the yeasty, earthy goodness of this cake, but whichever side you are on, you will enjoy this beautiful Bundt.

SERVES 10 TO 12

2 packages yeast
  (approximately 4½ teaspoons)
½ cup warm water
1 cup butter
5 cups sifted flour
1¼ cups sugar, divided
½ teaspoon salt

6 egg yolks
1 cup sour cream
8 ounces cream cheese, softened
2 eggs
1 teaspoon vanilla extract
¾ cup apricot preserves
Confectioners' sugar for dusting

Preheat oven to 350°F. Prepare a 12-cup Bundt pan using butter and flour or Baker's Joy and set aside.

Dissolve yeast in warm water and set aside in a warm place. Melt butter and set aside. Sift flour with ¾ cup of sugar and salt into a large bowl and set aside. Beat yolks until thick and lightly colored. Thoroughly blend in sour cream and butter. Stir in the dissolved yeast. Gradually stir yolk-yeast mixture into the dry ingredients. The dough should be soft and smooth. This can be easily done in a Kitchen-Aid mixer. Turn dough onto a floured board and knead until smooth and elastic, about 5 minutes. Put it in a lightly buttered bowl, and cover it with a clean tea towel or plastic wrap until almost doubled in bulk. This will take about 1½ hours.

To prepare the cheese filling, beat the cheese until light and fluffy. Blend in the remaining ½ cup of sugar, beating well. Add whole eggs one at a time, beating well after each addition. Stir in the vanilla. Set aside.

Punch down the dough and knead it a few times on a floured board. Roll the dough flat into a large circle, about 18 inches in diameter. Lay it over the prepared pan. Fit the dough in the pan, allowing it to hang over the sides. Pour in the cheese filling. Lift the edges of the dough over the filling and seal to inside ring of dough. Cut an X into the center of the ring and fold each of the four triangles back over the formed ring. Let it rise until the dough comes to the top of the pan, approximately 30 to 45 minutes.

Bake for 40 minutes or until golden brown. Let cool for 10 minutes and invert on a cooling rack or plate.

Heat the ¾ cup apricot preserves in a saucepan until the mixture thins. Drizzle this over the coffeecake and lightly dust with confectioners' sugar.

"I BELIEVE THAT AS LONG AS I KEEP BAKING, MY GRANDMOTHER HASN'T REALLY GONE. I BELIEVE BAKING IS THE BEST WAY FOR ME TO EXPRESS LOVE FOR MY PEOPLE IN THE PRESENT AND HONOR THE PEOPLE OF MY PAST, ALL IN ONE BATCH."
EMILY SMITH, NATIONAL PUBLIC RADIO, NOVEMBER 20, 2006

Harvest Bundts

Cranberry Orange Bundt

Low-Fat Apple Cake

Pumpkin Spice Cake

Peanut Butter and Jelly Bundt

Clementine Delight Bundt

In A Snap Banana Bundt

Apple Butter Bundt with Cider Glaze

White Fruitcake

Aunt Nettie's Orange Nut Cake

Apple Bundt

Banana Chiffon Bundt

Cranberry Orange Bundt

The Nordic Ware Company has declared November 15 "National Bundt Day." In honor of the proclamation, I created this new Bundt cake. Gorgeously made in the Cathedral Bundt pan, it is rich and citrusy to balance the sweet-tart filling. The finished cake looks like a poinsettia, making it a nice holiday dessert. Happy National Bundt Day to you and yours!

SERVES 10 TO 12

CAKE
2½ cups flour

2 teaspoons baking powder

1 teaspoon baking soda

1 teaspoon salt

1 cup butter, softened

1 cup sugar

3 eggs

1 teaspoon almond extract

1 cup sour cream

Grated zest of one orange

FILLING
8 ounces (half of a bag) fresh or frozen cranberries

½ cup water

⅔ cup sugar

½ teaspoon almond extract

¼ cup orange juice

LEMON-ORANGE GLAZE
¼ cup orange juice

Juice of ½ lemon

⅛ cup sugar

Preheat the oven to 350°F. Prepare a 12-cup Bundt pan using butter and flour or Baker's Joy and set aside.

Filling: Combine cranberries, sugar, water, almond extract, and orange juice in a small saucepan. Bring to a medium boil and cook, stirring constantly until the cranberries begin to pop and the mixture thickens. Remove from heat. Set aside 10 to 12 cranberries that are intact. Allow the mixture to cool to room temperature.

Cake: Combine flour, baking powder, baking soda, and salt. Set aside.

Beat the butter for several seconds in a large mixing bowl. Add the sugar and beat until smooth. Add the eggs and almond extract and beat for 2 to 3 minutes or until light and fluffy. Add the flour mixture and beat until smooth. Add the sour cream and orange zest and mix well.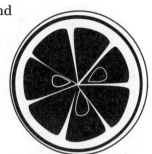

Pour ⅓ of the batter into the prepared pan. Gently spoon about ⅔ of the filling into the batter, taking care not to let the filling touch the sides of the pan. Spoon the remaining batter on top.

Bake for 55 to 60 minutes or until a toothpick comes out of the cake clean. Cool the cake in the pan for 10 minutes before inverting it onto a serving platter.

To prepare the glaze, place orange juice, lemon juice, and sugar in a small saucepan. Simmer on medium heat, stirring occasionally until the mixture thickens. Remove from heat until the cake is finished baking.

While the cake is still warm, gently brush on the orange-lemon glaze. When the cake is cool, spoon the remaining filling in between the flutes of the Cathedral Bundt. Gently press the whole cranberries (set aside from the glaze) in between the "cathedral windows." If you make the cake with a standard fluted Bundt, spoon the filling over the top and stud with the whole cranberries.

Low-Fat Apple Cake

I will be honest. I come from a people who don't do low-fat, don't know it, don't trust it, don't like it. My mother will deny it, but I have seen her put two table-spoons of butter in a pan to fry sausage. When I asked her about it, she looked at me as if I were crazy and said, "You have to get it started!" Most of my older relatives are fantastic bakers who will look at any recipe and say, "If you cannot fit another stick of butter or cup of sour cream into that recipe, you are simply not trying!" My genetic mistrust of low-fat is confirmed every time someone offers me a low-fat dessert that tastes like sawdust. I would rather have a smaller piece of cake or enjoy dessert less frequently than call something a treat that simply isn't.

But there are some really fantastic low-fat (not no-fat) desserts worth making, and this is one of them. I got this recipe from Flor-ence Schaller, a retired school teacher, volunteer at the Min-nesota Historical Society, and a really great person. When I was the caterer for the Macalester Plymouth United Church, it was my pleasure to work in the kitchen with Florence. This is a recipe that both your taste buds and waistline will enjoy.

SERVES 10 TO 12

3 cups flour

1½ cups sugar

1 teaspoon baking soda

1 teaspoon salt

1 teaspoon cinnamon

1 scant cup unsweetened
  applesauce

⅓ cup vegetable oil

3 eggs

1 teaspoon vanilla extract

3 medium apples, chopped
  (about 3 cups)

Preheat oven to 350°F. Prepare a 12-cup Bundt pan using butter and flour or Baker's Joy and set aside.

Combine dry ingredients and set aside. Mix applesauce, oil, eggs, and vanilla until smooth. Add dry ingredients and stir only until blended. Fold in chopped apples. Pour it into the prepared pan.

Bake for 1 hour or until a toothpick comes out of the cake clean. Let it cool in pan for 10 minutes, and then turn onto a serving plate or wire rack to finish cooling.

This luscious cake needs only a dusting of confectioners' sugar before serving. The applesauce, which replaces much of the fat, makes this cake moist and very satisfying.

"I COME FROM A FAMILY WHERE GRAVY IS CONSIDERED A BEVERAGE." ERMA BOMBECK

Pumpkin Spice Cake

This cake has just the right blend of rich pumpkin, autumn spices, and toasted walnuts. I developed this recipe after trying many others that I found lacking in various ways. Some tasted like pumpkin bread. Others had extraneous ingredients. The rest lacked zing. I like this recipe. I once catered food for the hospitality room at a political convention for a dear friend who was running for state office. I have a picture of the opposition's supporters (sporting rival t-shirts) slinking into our room to get slices of this Bundt. In the spirit of democracy, I offered them seconds.

SERVES 10 TO 12

¾ cup chopped toasted walnuts

1 cup vegetable oil

3 eggs

1 small can pumpkin puree (not pumpkin pie filling)

1 teaspoon vanilla extract

2 teaspoons bourbon

2½ cups flour

1 cup sugar

1 teaspoon baking powder

¼ teaspoon salt

1 teaspoon ground nutmeg

1 teaspoon ground allspice

1 teaspoon ground cinnamon

½ teaspoon ground cloves

Preheat oven to 350°F. Prepare a 12-cup Bundt pan using butter and flour or Baker's Joy and set aside.

Place chopped walnuts in a metal pan in the oven and toast for 10 to 15 minutes, taking care not to burn the nuts. Set them aside to cool. Beat together oil, eggs, pumpkin, vanilla, and bourbon. Sift together the flour, sugar, baking powder, salt, and spices. Add the flour mixture to the pumpkin mixture and mix until combined. Stir in the walnuts. Pour into the prepared pan.

Bake for 60 minutes or until a toothpick comes out of the cake clean. Let cool in pan for 10 minutes, then turn out onto a wire rack to cool completely.

Serve this with a dusting of confectioners' sugar or a dollop of freshly whipped cream (page 136).

"I DEFY ANYBODY TO PICK A FIGHT IN A KITCHEN THAT SMELLS OF BAKING PUMPKIN!" INTERNET BLOG

Peanut Butter and Jelly Bundt

Many years ago, I worked one summer at a day care center. During an open house, someone brought a PB & J layer cake. She told me that her husband always suggested she make it for nearly every event since kids like it so much. The children undoubtedly loved this, but so did he—and so did I, but I never got the recipe. This cake is my replication of the taste and feel of that layer cake in a Bundt. It has just the right balance of sweet and savory. My daughter and her neighborhood gang immediately devoured the first test cake I made with this recipe. I would love to tell you whether this cake keeps well, but it has never lasted long enough for me to know.

SERVES 10 TO 12

CAKE

2 cups flour

1 teaspoon baking soda

1 teaspoon salt

½ cup butter, softened

1 cup sugar

⅛ cup smooth peanut butter

1 teaspoon vanilla extract

2 eggs

1 cup buttermilk

¾ to 1 cup raspberry preserves

FROSTING

¼ cup butter, softened

¾ cup smooth peanut butter

1 teaspoon vanilla extract

2 cups sifted confectioners' sugar

3 to 4 tablespoons half-and-half

Preheat oven to 350°F. Prepare a 12-cup Bundt pan using butter and flour or Baker's Joy and set aside.

Combine flour, baking soda, and salt and set aside. Beat butter and sugar until fluffy. Add peanut butter, vanilla, and eggs and beat thoroughly. Add the flour mixture alternating with the buttermilk, combining well after each addition. Pour into the prepared pan.

Bake for 40 to 45 minutes or until a toothpick comes out of the cake clean. Allow the cake to cool in the pan for 10 minutes and invert onto a wire rack or serving platter to finish cooling.

To prepare the frosting, beat the butter until fluffy. Add the peanut butter and vanilla and combine thoroughly. Add the sugar alternating with the half-and-half until light and fluffy.

When the cake is cool, slice it horizontally with a serrated knife. Aim a little higher than halfway up. Flip the top half onto a plate and spread the raspberry preserves on the bottom half. Place the top half back on the cake. Frost the cake with peanut butter frosting (see page 136).

"WHAT IS PATRIOTISM BUT THE LOVE OF FOOD ONE ATE AS A CHILD?"

LIN YUTANG, WRITER AND TRANSLATOR

Clementine Delight Bundt

Gelatin is one of those dishes "foodies" will claim to dislike and then take a heaping serving at a church potluck. Gelatin eaters, come out of the closet! Don't be such a snob! Admit it's good! This Clementine Delight Bundt is pure comfort food: creamy and tangy with just a nudge of sweetness. It reminds me of one of my favorite childhood flavors, Bayer Children's Aspirin. I adapted this recipe from an old church cookbook, substituting fresh fruit for canned and using freshly whipped cream instead of store-bought whipped topping. I like to serve this for a winter brunch when clementines are widely available and most other fruits are not. If you are not in the mood to whip cream, commercially prepared whipped topping will work just fine.

SERVES 10 TO 12

1 clementine orange

1 (8 ounce) can crushed pineapple, undrained

2 tablespoons white sugar

1 (6 ounce) package orange-flavored gelatin

1 cup orange juice

2 cups buttermilk

2 cups heavy cream or 1 (8-ounce) container whipped topping

Lightly oil a 12-cup Bundt pan and set aside. Segment the clementine, remove any white pith, and cut each piece in half. Mix the pineapple, clementine segments, and sugar together in a medium saucepan. Bring mixture to a medium boil, stirring occasionally. Add the gelatin and stir until it is completely dissolved. Add the orange juice and continue stirring for another minute. Remove the mixture from the heat and cool to room temperature. Add the buttermilk and refrigerate at least 1 hour. The mixture should be partially set.

Prepare stabilized whipped cream on page 137. Whipping the cream works best if the mixing bowl and beaters are very cold. Gently fold the whipped cream into the gelatin mixture. Pour it into the prepared pan. Refrigerate for 6 to 8 hours, or until completely set.

Just prior to serving, dip the Bundt into a large bowl of warm water, taking care not to let water run onto gelatine mixture. Run a sharp knife gently around the edge of the pan and the center hole. Invert onto a serving platter. While this Bundt does not require additional sauces, I sometimes adorn the top with additional clementine segments or mandarin orange slices. If you use fresh oranges, make sure that you remove all of the white pith and add them just prior to serving.

"NO MATTER HOW MUCH JELL-O YOU PUT IN A SWIMMING POOL, YOU STILL CAN'T WALK ON WATER." UNKNOWN

In A Snap Banana Bundt

This cake almost makes itself. I swear a toddler could bake this cake as long as someone else preheated the oven. It is versatile and can be dressed up or down depending on your time and need. If you are squeamish about admitting to using cake mixes, you better figure out your lie, because you *will* be asked for this recipe. I adapted this from a recipe on an Internet message board. It reminds me of one that I used to look forward to at Methodist church potlucks growing up. I always tried to see who brought it to get the recipe, but I never did figure it out.

SERVES 10 TO 12

1 box (18-ounce) yellow cake mix

1 small box instant banana pudding mix

3 eggs

1 cup water

½ cup sour cream or yogurt

1 teaspoon vanilla extract

¼ cup vegetable oil

¾ cup mashed ripe bananas

½ cup chopped walnuts

Preheat over to 350°F. Prepare a 12-cup Bundt pan using butter and flour or Baker's Joy and set aside.

In a large bowl, mix together the cake and pudding mixes. Make a well in the center and pour in eggs, water, sour cream, vanilla, oil, and mashed bananas. Mix on low speed until blended and then mix on medium speed for 3 minutes until fluffy. Stir in walnuts. Spoon into prepared pan.

Bake for 50 to 55 minutes or until golden brown and firm to the touch. Let cool in pan for 10 minutes, then turn out onto a wire rack to cool completely.

This cake is delicious with a chocolate glaze (page 124) or chocolate buttercream (page 133). I also like it plain, with just a dusting of confectioners' sugar. If you want to avoid a dry-looking exterior, slather the warm cake with honey butter (page 126) to give it a luscious glow. This cake is also good with a scoop of high-quality vanilla ice cream. Don't forget a strong cup of coffee.

 THE AMAZING BANANA LEAF!

Consider dressing up your Banana Bundt with banana leaves cut into squares or other shapes, and draped over individual dessert plates. It makes a lovely presentation that can be done ahead. This is especially nice for the finish to an Asian meal. You can purchase fresh banana leaves at most Asian markets. When you get them they are a dull green, but a simple procedure will turn them bright and glossy. Take the banana leaf (which is impossibly large!) and pass it quickly over the flame on a gas stove. They turn a beautiful shiny jungle green.

"DURING THE PAST YEAR, I'VE BECOME VERY POPULAR AT WORK. NOT FOR MY BRAINS. NOT FOR MY BEAUTY. FOR MY BUNDT PANS. EVERY WEEK, I BAKE A NEW CAKE FOR MY COLLEAGUES. WHY CAKE? BECAUSE COOKIES ARE TOO JUVENILE. WHY MONDAY? BECAUSE NO MATTER HOW MUCH YOU LOVE YOUR JOB, MONDAY IS THE DAY YOU LOOK FORWARD TO LEAST. A SLICE OF CAKE MAKES IT BETTER."

MELISSA GRAY, NATIONAL PUBLIC RADIO, OCTOBER 11, 2006

Apple Butter Bundt with Cider Glaze

My mother found this recipe in an old church cookbook she picked up at a garage sale. It is pure comfort food, rich and sweet with nutty undertones. The original recipe called for a corn-syrup glaze that I thought overpowered the cake. I developed an apple cider glaze that complements the cake, but still lets it be the star. Think of this Bundt when the leaves are nearly down and there is a crisp chill in the air. The cake fits in snugly with a simple supper of soup and bread. This recipe also works well with pear butter.

SERVES 10 TO 12

CAKE

8 ounces cream cheese, softened

½ cup softened butter

1⅛ cups sugar

5 eggs

1 cup apple butter

1 teaspoon vanilla extract

2 teaspoons bourbon

2 cups flour

1½ teaspoons baking powder

1 teaspoon cinnamon

½ teaspoon salt

1 cup chopped pecans

GLAZE

1 cup apple cider (not apple juice)

2 tablespoons honey

Juice of ½ lemon

¼ cup sugar

½ teaspoon corn starch

½ cup confectioners' sugar

Preheat oven to 350°F. Prepare a 12-cup Bundt pan using butter and flour or Baker's Joy and set aside.

Beat together cream cheese, butter, and sugar in a large bowl until light and fluffy. Add the eggs one at a time, beating thoroughly after each addition. Combine apple butter, vanilla, and bourbon and set aside. Combine flour, baking powder, cinnamon, and salt and set aside. Add the flour and the apple butter mixtures alternately to the cream cheese-butter-sugar mixture, combining well after each addition. Stir in the nuts. Pour the batter into the prepared pan.

Bake for 50 to 60 minutes or until a toothpick comes out of the cake clean. Cool in the pan for 15 minutes before inverting onto a cooling rack or serving plate.

To prepare the glaze, place apple cider, honey, lemon juice, and sugar in a small saucepan. Bring mixture to a rolling boil. Reduce the heat to maintain a low boil and stir constantly until the mixture thickens slightly, about 5 minutes. Remove 2 tablespoons of the cider mixture and thoroughly dissolve the corn starch in it. Return it to the saucepan and continue to cook until mixture thickens further, about 4 minutes. Add ½ cup confectioners' sugar and cook until the glaze is thick enough to be spooned over the cake, about 4 minutes. Brush glaze over the hot cake. This process will use about ⅔ of the glaze. When the cake is cooled, spoon the remaining glaze over the cake. It will have thickened considerably, giving it the appearance of honey.

This cake needs nothing other than the glaze. It is also good served only with a dusting of confectioners' sugar and a dollop of ginger-scented whipped cream (page 137).

 A HAIKU MOMENT—JUST FOR YOU

The Bundt, it was dry.

He glazed and frosted and fussed.

Next time, add the eggs.

White Fruitcake

My grandmother brought her fruitcake recipe to the United States from Cornwall, England, in 1924. Her cake is lighter and retains moisture better then most fruitcakes. On Christmas Eve, she always made this cake and bread pudding and quoted Tiny Tim by saying, "God bless us, everyone." That famous line still brings a lump to my throat. The Christmas before she passed away, she was too sick to do her holiday baking, but she sat in a chair and coached my grandfather through making this cake.

SERVES 10 TO 12

2 cups flour

½ teaspoon baking soda

1 teaspoon baking powder

⅛ cup candied citrus peel

1 cup fine coconut

1 cup white raisins

½ cup candied red cherries, cut in half

1 ring each of candied red, yellow, and
    green pineapple, finely chopped

1 cup butter, softened

1 cup white sugar

3 eggs

1¼ cup buttermilk

1 cup slivered almonds

Preheat oven to 300°F. Prepare a 12-cup Bundt pan using butter and flour or Baker's Joy and set aside.

Combine flour, baking soda, and baking powder. Add citrus peel, coconut, raisins, cherries, and pineapple and set aside. Beat butter and sugar until fluffy. Add eggs one at a time, beating after each addition. Alternately add buttermilk and flour mixture to the butter, mixing well after each addition. Stir in almonds. Pour the batter into the prepared Bundt pan.

Bake for 3 hours or until a toothpick comes out of the cake clean.

This cake is best made 2 to 3 weeks prior to the holidays. Wrap it in foil and store it in a tin with a tightly fitting lid to thoroughly season.

"WHAT KEEPS ME MOTIVATED IS NOT THE FOOD ITSELF BUT ALL THE BONDS AND MEMORIES THE FOOD REPRESENTS."
MICHAEL CHIARELLO, COOKBOOK AUTHOR AND CHEF

Aunt Nettie's Orange Nut Cake

My great-great Aunt Nettie, born in 1867, had a very difficult life and died when she was quite young. My 92-year-old grandmother remembers her as a fantastic cook and a generous woman who brought presents, love, and cake (often this one) to their otherwise spartan holiday celebrations. Some families have trust funds to hold them together; mine has recipes. When I make this cake I feel connected to this woman, whom I never met.

My original recipe calls for grinding an entire orange. When I asked my grandma how to do this, she said just use the hand grinder that you use for meat. Naturally!

I have adapted this recipe for using a food processor. I also sometimes substitute dried cranberries for the raisins. This is a dense cake that really packs a punch.

SERVES 10 TO 12

1 cup raisins or dried cranberries

1 ground orange—peel and fruit

¼ cup hot water

1½ cups flour

1 teaspoon baking soda

½ teaspoon salt

1½ cups sugar

½ cup butter, softened

2 eggs

¾ cup buttermilk

¾ cup nuts, finely chopped

Preheat oven to 350°F. Prepare a 12-cup Bundt pan using butter and flour or Baker's Joy and set aside.

Place the raisins and the coarsely chopped orange in a food processor and pulse until the mixture is finely ground. Pour the ¼ cup hot water over the mixture and set aside. Combine flour, baking soda, and salt in a large bowl and set aside. Beat sugar and butter in a large bowl until light and fluffy. Add the eggs one at a time, mixing well after each addition. Alternately add the flour ingredients and the buttermilk to the sugar-butter mixture until smooth. Stir in the orange-raisin mixture and the nuts. Pour the batter into the prepared Bundt pan.

Bake for 45 to 50 minutes or until a toothpick comes out of the cake clean. Allow the cake to cool in the pan for 10 minutes before inverting it onto a wire rack or serving platter to cool completely.

This is a very dense cake that needs only a dusting of confectioners' sugar before serving. It also works well with fluffy butter vanilla frosting (page 132).

DOES ANYONE KNOW WHAT THIS MEANS?
"SOMEONE LEFT THE CAKE OUT IN THE RAIN.
I DON'T THINK THAT I CAN TAKE IT.
'CAUSE IT TOOK SO LONG TO BAKE IT.
AND I'LL NEVER HAVE THAT RECIPE AGAIN."
MACARTHUR PARK, JIMMY WEBB, COMPOSER

Apple Bundt

My publisher sent me this recipe with a note that said, "Like apple pie—the best Bundt I've ever made." It seemed only prudent to test his claim and include the recipe. This is indeed a very moist Bundt with deep apple flavor not drowned in too much sugar. The recipe is from the Epicurious.com website, and I adapted it to bring out a little more of the tart side of apples. This goes well with a pumpkin-carving party or a fall planning meeting.

SERVES 10 TO 12

5 medium apples (Granny Smith and some Macintosh or Gala),
    peeled and cut into small pieces

2½ cups plus 5 tablespoons sugar

2 teaspoons ground cinnamon

½ teaspoon mace

1 tablespoon freshly squeezed lemon juice

3 cups flour

3 teaspoons baking powder

½ teaspoon salt

1 cup vegetable oil

4 large eggs

¼ cup orange juice

1 tablespoon orange peel

1 teaspoon vanilla extract

Preheat oven to 350°F. Prepare a 12-cup Bundt pan using butter and flour or Baker's Joy and set aside.

Mix apple pieces, 5 tablespoons of sugar, cinnamon, mace, and lemon juice and set aside. Blend flour, baking powder, and salt and set aside. Combine 2½ cups sugar, oil, eggs, orange juice, orange peel, and vanilla in a large bowl. Thoroughly stir the flour mixture into the egg mixture. Alternate the batter and the apples in 3 layers beginning and ending with batter.

Bake for about 1½ hours or until a toothpick comes out of the cake clean. Cool the cake in the pan for 10 minutes before inverting onto a cooling rack for an hour.

This is a dense cake that will become too heavy if you cool it on the serving platter. It is sturdy enough to withstand being moved.

Don't overshadow this cake with anything too weighty. Try dusting with confectioners' sugar, or spreading the surface with some honey butter glaze (page 126). This fresh-tasting cake is also very good with a dollop of whipped cream or a scoop of good-quality vanilla ice cream.

 A VARIETY OF APPLES

My mother taught me that the best apple pies and cakes have more than one kind of apple in them, because the varieties complement each other with differing levels of tartness, firmness, and moisture. Sure enough, when I lived on an apple orchard in Pennsylvania, my landlord would bring me combinations of apples for my baking. He knew each variety intimately, and the quality of my apple baking that year proved my mother was right. Try pairing Granny Smith, Cortland, and Gala apples for a great blend of sweetness and texture.

Banana Chiffon Bundt

My 11-year-old niece adapted this from a recipe she found in a 1955 *Good Housekeeping Cookbook*. Whenever I hear people say that no one cooks anymore, I think of my niece and my 10-year-old daughter, who can quickly turn out a delicious pie, cake, or cookie.

This is a light, flavorful cake that works well with a number of finishing touches. My niece likes to serve this elegant cake with grilled bananas, a standard dessert in her mother's native Vietnam. This sophisticated cake makes a perfect ending to a dinner party.

SERVES 10 TO 12

7 egg yokes unbeaten

7 egg whites

2 cups sifted all-purpose flour

1½ cups granulated sugar

3 teaspoons baking powder

1 teaspoon salt

½ cup vegetable oil

2 mashed ripe bananas

1 tablespoon lemon juice

½ teaspoon cream of tartar

Preheat oven to 325°F. Prepare a 12-cup Bundt pan using butter and flour or Baker's Joy and set aside.

Bring eggs to room temperature by allowing them to sit in warm water, then separate the whites and yolks. Sift flour, sugar, baking powder, and salt into a large electric mixing bowl. Make a well in the flour mixture and pour the vegetable oil into the well. Add egg yolks, bananas, and lemon juice and beat until smooth. In another large bowl, combine egg whites and cream of tartar. Beat the egg whites until they hold very stiff peaks. Do not underbeat. A whisk attachment to your mixer is useful for this task. Slowly pour the egg yolk mixture over the whites, folding in gently with a rubber spatula. Continue folding until yolk mixture is just blended and you no longer see white streaks. Pour the batter into the prepared pan.

Bake for 55 to 65 minutes or until a toothpick comes out of the cake clean. Cool for 10 minutes in the pan and invert onto a wire rack to finish cooling.

This cake is beautiful with just a dusting of confectioners' sugar. If you do not like the look of a dry exterior, gently coat the surface of the warm cake with honey butter glaze (page 126). It also works well with vanilla buttercream icing. This is especially elegant served with grilled bananas.

 ## GRILLED BANANAS

Grilling bananas is a tasty thing to do when you are already planning to grill. After your other grilling is completed, simply throw the bananas on the rack and lower the lid. Allow the bananas to roast until the skins are deep black and the banana is soft and almost caramelized. For a variation, slit the skin and insert small pieces of high-quality chocolate into the banana. When the roasting is complete, the result is a sweet gooey, ethereal mass.

Springtime Bundts

Carrot Cake

Great St. Louis Orange Ring Cake

Pistachio Bundt

Rave Reviews Cake

Quick Orange Kiss Bundt

Coconut Swirl Cake with Easter Jellybeans

Lemonade Cake

Pineapple Upside-Down Cake

Over-the-Rainbow Ice Cream Mold

Carrot Cake

I love a good carrot cake. It is moist and bursting with nuts, raisins, and spices. Plus, you can eat that second piece secure in the knowledge that you are eating a vegetable. This is my mother's recipe, and she adds a little pineapple to give it a nudge of sweetness. A friend of mine finds this practice to be a form of heresy. You choose. With or without the pineapple, you are going to like this Bundt!

This makes an adorable Easter cake topped with cream cheese frosting and decorated with tiny gummy bunnies, gummy chicks, and miniature jelly beans.

SERVES 10 TO 12

1½ cups finely grated carrots (easy to do with a food processor)

1 tablespoon lemon juice

½ cup crushed pineapple

1⅓ cups all-purpose flour

1 cup sugar

1 teaspoon baking powder

1 teaspoon baking soda

½ teaspoon salt

¾ teaspoon cinnamon

½ teaspoon cloves

½ teaspoon nutmeg or mace

½ teaspoon allspice

¾ cup vegetable oil

3 eggs

1 cup raisins (golden look especially nice)

1 cup chopped walnuts

Preheat oven to 350°F. Prepare a 12-cup Bundt pan using butter and flour or Baker's Joy and set aside.

Combine grated carrots, lemon juice, and pineapple in a small bowl and set aside. Combine the flour, sugar, baking powder, baking soda, salt, and spices in a large mixing bowl. Add oil and beat until smooth. Add eggs one at a time, beating after each addition. Add the carrot mixture and mix well. Stir in raisins and walnuts. Pour into the prepared pan.

Bake for 55 to 60 minutes or until a toothpick comes out of the cake clean. Cool for 10 minutes in the pan and invert on a rack or serving platter to cool thoroughly.

Many people expect cream cheese frosting (page 134) with their carrot cake, and it does complement the cake nicely. When I have made this carrot cake for dairy intolerant individuals, I slather the warm cake with honey butter glaze (page 126) or dust with confectioners' sugar.

 ### FRESH SPICES

I have a friend who buys her spices in bulk. This is a great idea since you can buy only what you need and don't waste anything. The problem? She keeps the spices longer than husbands. Stale and unlabeled, the spices are difficult to identify! I encourage you to buy high-quality spices in small enough quantities that they will be fresh and vibrant when you need them. If you cannot identify a spice by its smell, it's time to go to the store for more.

"VEGETABLES ARE A MUST ON A DIET. I SUGGEST CARROT CAKE, ZUCCHINI BREAD, AND PUMPKIN PIE." JIM DAVIS, *GARFIELD* COMIC STRIP

Great St. Louis Orange Ring Cake with Orange-Lemon Syrup

I've borrowed this recipe from Richard Sax's *Classic Home Desserts: A Treasury of Heirloom and Contemporary Recipes from Around the World*. If you don't own this book, put it on your birthday list immediately. I honor him and his work every time I open his book, which is filled with wonderful, beautiful recipes for any occasion. I once made this cake for a political gathering, and as I set the cake down on the table, the 14-year-old daughter of the host shook her head and said, "You are nuts being a caterer. If I ever made anything that beautiful, I would kill the person who tried to eat it."

SERVES 10 TO 12

CAKE

1¾ cups flour

1 teaspoon baking soda

1 teaspoon baking powder

1 cup butter, softened

1 cup sugar

Grated zest of 1 orange

3 large eggs, separated

1 cup low-fat plain yogurt

1½ teaspoons vanilla extract

A pinch of salt

SYRUP

Juice of 1 large orange

Juice of 1 lemon

½ cup sugar

pinch of salt

Preheat oven to 325°F. Prepare a 12-cup Bundt pan using butter and flour or Baker's Joy and set aside.

Sift together the flour, baking soda, and baking powder and set aside. Beat the butter until light and fluffy. Slowly add the sugar and orange zest and continue beating until the sugar is dissolved and the mixture is very light, about 6 minutes. Add the egg yolks, yogurt, and vanilla and beat until light and fluffy. Lower the speed and add the flour mixture, taking care not to over mix. In a separate bowl, beat egg whites that have been brought to room temperature with the salt until stiff, but not dry. Fold them into the batter just until blended. Pour the batter into the prepared pan and smooth the surface.

Bake about 1 hour or until a toothpick comes out of the cake clean. Cool for 10 minutes and invert on a plate. Spoon or brush the cake with the hot syrup.

To make the orange syrup, combine orange juice, lemon juice, sugar, and salt in a saucepan. Bring to a boil and then gently simmer until mixture thickens, about 8 minutes.

This cake needs no adornment other than the orange syrup. It is especially beautiful in a Cathedral Bundt pan.

"A GOOD COOK IS LIKE A SORCERESS WHO DISPENSES HAPPINESS."
ELSA SCHIAPARELLI, *SHOCKING LIFE* (1954)

Pistachio Bundt

If you were hoping to find an elegant Mediterranean Bundt with roasted pistachios, olive oil, and honey, look elsewhere. This is a weird, bright green 1970s cake. I found the clipping in a big box of my mother's recipes. When my mother leaves this earth, it will take months to sort through them. She has recipes on napkins, post-it notes, and, my personal favorite, funeral bulletins—even my grandmother's. (Was Mom even listening to the meditation?)

I once made this retro Bundt for a '70s party, and it looked great next to the Jell-O molds, pigs-in-a-blanket, and Cheez-whiz on a Ritz. Don't be alarmed by the unnatural color; it is part of the charm.

SERVES 10 TO 12

1 box (18-ounce) yellow cake mix

1 small box instant pistachio pudding mix

4 eggs

¾ cup orange juice

½ cup vegetable oil

1 cup drained crushed pineapple

½ cup coconut

Preheat oven to 350°F. Prepare a 12-cup Bundt pan using butter and flour or Baker's Joy and set aside.

Combine the cake and pudding mixes in a large bowl. Add eggs, orange juice, and oil and beat at medium speed for 4 minutes. Add the pineapple and coconut and stir until blended. Pour into the prepared pan.

Bake for 55 to 60 minutes or until a toothpick comes out of the cake clean. Allow the cake to cool in the pan for 10 minutes and invert to a rack or serving plate to finish cooling.

I don't like to interfere with the green shade of this cake by using a heavy frosting or glaze. I either brush the Bundt with a simple lime syrup (page 128) or a dusting of confectioners' sugar. This also works great for Saint Patrick's Day!

"PART OF THE SECRET OF SUCCESS IN LIFE IS TO EAT WHAT YOU LIKE AND LET THE FOOD FIGHT IT OUT INSIDE." MARK TWAIN, HUMORIST

Rave Reviews Cake

More than one family member and friend sent me this recipe when they learned I was writing this book. The recipe is originally from the back of the Baker's Angel Coconut package. Easy, easy, easy. When I kitchen-tested it, I got a ringing endorsement from my two-year-old son. The finished cake was sitting on the counter, ready for our dinner guests. I stepped away to let the dog outside, and when I returned to the kitchen, there was a gaping hole in the cake, and crumbs and goo on my son's face. He took one look at my face and said, "I said I was sorry. I love you so much, Mama!" I served it anyway, and everyone loved it, hole and all.

SERVES 10 TO 12

1 box (18-ounce) yellow cake mix

1 small box vanilla instant pudding mix

1⅓ cups water

4 eggs

¼ cup oil

1⅓ cup coconut

1 cup chopped walnuts

Preheat oven to 325°F. Prepare a 12-cup Bundt pan using butter and flour or Baker's Joy and set aside.

Combine cake and pudding mixes, water, eggs, and oil in a large bowl. Beat on medium speed for 4 minutes. Stir in the coconut and nuts. Pour into the prepared pan.

Bake 1 hour or until a toothpick comes out of the cake clean. Cool for 15 minutes and invert onto a cooling rack or serving platter.

This is delicious with caramel frosting (page 133). It also works well with fluffy coconut frosting (page 135).

 TAKING FOOD TO NEIGHBORS

One of the tasks my mother gave me at an early age was bringing cookies or slices of cakes and pies to several older single people in our neighborhood. This taught me the value of sharing and helped me learn how to interact respectfully with different kinds of people. I am on a one-woman campaign to bring back this community-building habit! The next time you make a pot of soup or a special treat, share it with somebody else. Don't wait for a family illness, death, or birth of a baby; a "just because" pot of soup or a slab of warm pie makes living on this planet a little more pleasant.

Quick Orange Kiss Bundt

This cake was a big hit at a church supper I catered, despite the unexpected "secret ingredient" added by my two-year-old son! He was "helping" me in the kitchen, standing on a chair next to the mixer, decked out in his special firefighter apron. Then came the evil grin. Before I could respond, he tossed two handfuls of cheddar cheese goldfish crackers into the batter! They were pulverized in seconds. Not having time to start over, I served the cakes with a smile. No one suspected, although one woman did say she liked the distinct contrast of sweet and savory in it! With or without the little carp, this cake is a winner—moist and light and perfect for an after-school snack or picnic supper.

SERVES 10 TO 12

1 box (18-ounce) yellow cake mix
1 small box instant lemon pudding mix
¾ cup orange juice
½ cup vegetable oil
4 eggs
1 tablespoon lemon juice

Preheat oven to 325°F. Prepare a 12-cup Bundt pan using butter and flour or Baker's Joy and set aside.

In a large mixing bowl, combine the cake and pudding mixes. Add orange juice, oil, eggs, and lemon juice. Beat 4 minutes on medium speed. Pour into the prepared pan.

Bake for 50 to 60 minutes or until a toothpick comes out of the cake clean. Let cool in pan for 10 minutes, then turn out onto a wire rack to cool completely.

This cake is best served with an orange glaze (page 129), or with freshly whipped cream or a scoop of high-quality vanilla ice cream.

MAKE MINE À LA MODE

Many people like ice cream with their Bundt cakes, and why not? Sometimes, however, poorly presented ice cream can ruin the good looks of a slice of Bundt. I have a remedy for this that will also make serving a breeze.

The morning before a dinner party, set out the ice cream to thaw slightly, about 5 minutes. Using a small ice cream scoop, make as many balls of ice cream as you will need. Take time to make them uniform and attractive. Place them on a cookie sheet and return them to the freezer. When they are hardened, put them in a resealable freezer bag. Serve them decoratively placed alongside the Bundt cake. Voilà!

Coconut Swirl Cake with Easter Jellybeans

An Easter cake, light and flavorful, with coconut frosting reminiscent of lamb's wool. My grandmother used to make a lamb cake with frosting wool and jellybean eyes, and my brother and I used to vie for the honor of making it into a "Cyclops" lamb. This Bundt is the grown-up version of that cake. For an extra touch, set the cake on a bed of green tinted coconut.

SERVES 10 TO 12

6 large egg yolks

1 cup milk, divided

2 teaspoons vanilla extract

2 cups cake flour

1½ cup sugar

1 tablespoon baking powder

½ teaspoon salt

12 tablespoons butter, softened

Preheat oven to 350°F. Prepare a 12-cup Bundt pan using butter and flour or Baker's Joy and set aside.

In a medium bowl combine egg yolks, ¼ cup milk, and vanilla. Set aside. Combine the flour, sugar, baking powder, and salt, and mix on medium for 30 seconds. Add the butter and remaining ¾ cup milk. Mix to moisten on low; turn the mixer to medium and beat for 2 minutes. Scrape down the sides. Add the egg mixture in 3 batches, beating well after each addition. Pour the batter into the prepared pans.

Bake for 40 minutes or until a toothpick comes out of the cake clean. Cool for 10 minutes and invert on a wire rack to finish cooling.

Slather with honey butter glaze (page 126) when the cake is still warm. Or, when it is cool, frost with fluffy coconut frosting (page 135).

 TINTED COCONUT

The Easter coconut cake looks particularly engaging on a green bed of coconut grass. To tint the coconut, take 1 cup flake coconut and toss it lightly with 4 drops of green food coloring. If you desire a deeper hue, add more food coloring, one drop at a time, until you reach your desired color.

Lemonade Cake

Intense sweetness paired with powerful sourness, and the smells and feelings of summer! My mother sent this recipe to me, passed along from a friend who got it from the *Des Moines County Register*. I made it for a Parent-Teacher Council cakewalk where it was a big hit.

SERVES 10 TO 12

1 small box lemon-flavored gelatin

¾ cup hot water

1 box (18-ounce) lemon cake mix

4 eggs

½ cup oil

1 (6-ounce) can frozen lemonade concentrate

½ cup sugar

Preheat oven to 325°F. Prepare a 12-cup Bundt pan using butter and flour or Baker's Joy and set aside.

Combine gelatin mix with water and set aside.

Thoroughly combine cake mix, eggs, and oil. Add the gelatin mixture and beat for 3 minutes.

Pour into the prepared pan.

Bake for 50 to 55 minutes or until a toothpick comes out of the cake clean. Allow the cake to cool for 15 minutes in the pan.

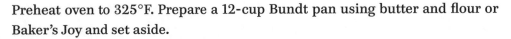

Combine the lemonade concentrate with the sugar. After the cake has cooled 15 minutes, gently loosen it from the sides of the pan. Pour ⅔ of the lemonade mixture over the cake in the pan, allowing it to run down the sides. Wait 10 minutes and invert the cake onto a serving platter. Pour the remaining lemonade mixture over the top of the cake.

"THE BUNDT PAN, WITH ITS TRADEMARK HOLE IN THE CENTER, IS A THING THAT FILLED A NEED—A VOID—NO ONE QUITE KNEW EXISTED." HANK STUEVER, *WASHINGTON POST*, JANUARY 11, 2005

Pineapple Upside-Down Cake

This recipe modifies my mother-in-law's pineapple upside-down cake recipe. It is quick to make and impressive, but it is a very sweet cake that would put most diabetics in a coma, so know your guest list! The confection goes wonderfully with a cup of strong black coffee. My daughter made it for her grandmother, who was appropriately impressed when my nine-year-old, bursting with pride, set it on the table. This scene reminded me of myself 25 years ago, when my own grandmother asked me to make the gravy for our Thanksgiving dinner. She was involved in the last-minute bustle of getting the feast to the table and was probably just happy for an extra set of hands. For me it was a rite of passage.

SERVES 10 TO 12

1 can pineapple rings with juice

1 box (18-ounce) yellow cake mix

12 tablespoons melted butter

3 eggs

½ cup brown sugar

½ cup butter

1 cup of pecan halves

1 jar maraschino cherries

Preheat oven to 350°F. Prepare a 12-cup Bundt pan using butter and flour or Baker's Joy and set aside.

Drain pineapple rings, reserving the juice and set aside. Thoroughly combine cake mix, melted butter, eggs, and 1 cup of the reserved pineapple juice. Beat for 3 minutes or until light and fluffy. Melt ½ cup butter. Add the brown sugar to the melted butter and mix thoroughly. Sprinkle this into the Bundt Pan. Place the pineapple rings around the inside of the Bundt. Place the pecans around the pineapple rings and maraschino cherries inside the pineapple rings. Carefully pour the batter into the prepared pan.

Bake for 45 to 50 minutes or until a toothpick comes out of the cake clean. Cool for 10 minutes and invert onto a serving platter.

The beauty of this cake is that it comes out finished! Serve warm or at room temperature.

"ONE OF THE REASONS MAKING CAKES IS SATISFYING IS THAT THE EFFORT REQUIRED IS SO MUCH LESS THAN THE GRATITUDE CONFERRED. . . . THE RETURNS ARE HIGH: YOU FEEL DISPROPORTIONATELY GOOD ABOUT YOURSELF AFTERWARDS."

NIGELLA LAWSON, *HOW TO BE A DOMESTIC GODDESS* (2001)

Over-the-Rainbow Ice Cream Mold

I adapted this from Dorothy Dalquist's *Over 300 Ways to Use Your Bundt Pan*. It is an elegant do-ahead dessert that looks as if you spent a lot of time on it. It also solves one of my personal dilemmas: nearly everyone likes ice cream, but I feel like such a slacker serving it! I fear my guests will know all I did was scoop it out of a container and into a bowl! But when you slice into this beauty, your guests know you thought about them and took the time to make something special. The beautiful pastel shades work especially well for a baby-shower brunch. Serve this alone or with a raspberry sauce and freshly whipped cream.

SERVES 10–12

½ gallon of high-quality vanilla ice cream

1 pint raspberry sherbet

1 pint lime sherbet

1 pint orange sherbet

1 cup fresh raspberries or sliced strawberries or

1 cup chopped nuts (optional)

Soften about half of the vanilla ice cream by beating it with a mixer. Spread half of it in the bottom of a 12-cup Bundt pan. Place the remaining softened ice cream back in the freezer. Using a small ice cream scoop or melon baller, make small mounds of sherbet and place them onto a platter. Work quickly to avoid the sherbet softening too much. Alternately place balls of sherbet in the pan. After you have one layer, sprinkle half of the fruit (and nuts) evenly over the sherbet. Place another layer of sherbet balls in the pan. Sprinkle the remaining fruit (and nuts) over the sherbet. Place another layer of sherbet balls in the pan. Spread the remaining softened vanilla ice cream over the sherbet. Using a spoon, flatten the mixture to eliminate any air bubbles in the pan. Cover with foil or plastic wrap and store in the freezer until you are ready to serve.

Just prior to serving, dip the Bundt into a large bowl of warm water. Take a sharp knife and gently run it around the edge of the pan and the center hole. Invert onto a serving platter. While this display needs no additional adornment, fresh strawberries or raspberries scattered on the platter add a lovely touch.

 JUST ASK!

Many people are lactose intolerant or allergic to dairy products. My spouse has this affliction, and there is nothing worse then going to a dinner party where you cannot eat the dessert! The best course of action is to ask your guests before the event if they have any allergies and alter the menu accordingly. Several good soy "ice cream" products and delicious sorbets are available in most supermarkets. A few years ago, I nearly made my sister-in-law cry by serving her a dairy-free milk shake. It only takes a second to ask and a few minutes to modify your plan to really make someone feel nurtured and included.

Bundts Off the Beaten Path

- -

Pine Nut and Chili Bundt

Saffron Cake

Eastern European Honey Cake

Green Chili Cornbread

Orange Pecan Beer Cake

Two Moons Wild Rice Bundt Cake

Coming Out Bundt

Strawberry Pretzel Bundt

- -

Pine Nut and Chili Bundt with Chili Glaze

While writing this book, my family and I moved to Santa Fe, New Mexico. I had great fun exploring a new place and its cuisine. The inspiration for this recipe came late one night when sleep would not. In my mind, it seemed that rich pine nuts and spicy ground chilies would be a fantastic combination in a pound cake. I was right. Serve this one for dessert after a Mexican or Tex-Mex meal. It also works well for a winter brunch. The lime-chili glaze provides a perfect contrast with the buttery cake and spicy filling. Fear not, I toned down the quantity of chilies. This will make your Scandinavian friends say, "More, please," not "Well, that's different!"

SERVES 10 TO 12

CAKE

¾ cup pine nuts

1½ tablespoons ground red chilies

½ teaspoon cinnamon

1 tablespoon sugar

2½ cups flour

2 teaspoons baking powder

1 teaspoon baking soda

1 teaspoon salt

1 cup softened butter

1 cup sugar

3 eggs

1 teaspoon vanilla extract

1 cup sour cream

GLAZE

Juice of 1 lemon

1 tablespoon honey

2 tablespoons sugar

1 teaspoon ground red chilies

Preheat oven to 350°F. Prepare a 12-cup Bundt pan using butter and flour or Baker's Joy and set aside.

Put the pine nuts in a pie pan and toast in the oven for 10 minutes or until lightly browned. Cool. Combine the toasted pine nuts, ground chilies, cinnamon, and sugar in a food processor. Pulse until the pine nuts are ground and the mixture is crumbly. Set aside.

Combine flour, baking powder, baking soda, and salt in a bowl. Set aside. Beat the butter for several seconds in a large mixing bowl. Add the sugar and beat until smooth. Add the eggs and vanilla extract and beat for 2 to 3 minutes or until light and fluffy. Add the flour mixture and beat until smooth. Add the sour cream and mix well. Pour half of the batter into the prepared pan. Scatter half of the pine nut mixture over the batter, taking care to distribute it evenly. Stir the remaining pine nut mixture into the remaining batter and spread that in the pan.

Bake for 1 hour or until a toothpick comes out of the cake clean. Cool for 10 minutes and invert on to a wire rack or plate.

To prepare the glaze, place lemon juice, honey, sugar, and ground chilies in a saucepan and bring to a boil. Reduce the heat and continue cooking until the mixture thickens, about 4 minutes.

Spoon or brush the cake with the glaze and serve slightly warm or at room temperature. If you choose to serve this cake pre-sliced, lightly dust the plate with a sprinkling of ground chilies. Place the cake on the plate and scatter a few pine nuts over the top.

Saffron Cake

This flavorful cake is more like bread. It has divided my family ever since my grandmother set foot in America. Some crave it, others despise it. I belong to the first group. The smell alone can make me salivate and put the kettle on for Earl Grey tea. This cake can dry out easily, so keep it well covered and eat it while it is fresh. I have been known to eat half a cake in an afternoon, one tiny sliver at a time.

SERVES 10 TO 12

6 cups of flour

1 teaspoon salt

½ cup plus 1 teaspoon sugar, divided

2½ teaspoons yeast

½ cup warm water

3 drams saffron (2 big pinches)

½ cup boiling water

½ teaspoon almond extract

1½ cups warm milk

2 cups shortening (I use half lard)

1 cup white raisins

1 cup black raisins

⅔ cup currants

Preheat oven to 350°F. Prepare a 12-cup Bundt pan using butter and flour or Baker's Joy and set aside.

Combine flour, salt, and ½ cup sugar and set aside. Dissolve yeast and 1 teaspoon sugar in ½ cup warm water and set aside until it is foamy. Steep saffron in boiling water and set aside. Dissolve the almond extract in warm milk. Add the shortening to the flour mixture and, using a pastry blender, mix until it is crumbly. Add raisins and currents. Add yeast, saffron, and warm milk and thoroughly combine. Do not knead. Place in the prepared Bundt pan and let rise until double.

Bake for 1 hour and 15 minutes or until a toothpick comes out of the cake clean.

This cake does not need any finishing. Simply cut it in slabs and serve for high tea with tiny sandwiches, fruit, and cream.

 WORKING WITH YEAST

People freak out about yeast. I am asking you to calm down and realize that, if you follow a couple of rules, you can produce beautiful yeast-based baked goods.

1. The water should be warm—about 100–115 degrees. Dribble some on the back of your hand—it should feel pleasant, not cold and not hot. If you are proofing your yeast (combining it first with water), you will know if it is not living. After about 5 minutes it should be foamy with an earthy yeasty smell. If it is not dissolving thoroughly, the water was too cold. If it remains lifeless and flat, the water was too hot. I like to proof the yeast in a metal bowl and float it over warm water in the sink. This is handy when your kitchen is cold—as is often the case in Minnesota!

2. Add a little sugar (½ to 1 teaspoon) to the water and yeast. This will give the yeast something to munch on as it multiplies.

3. Don't overproof the yeast. Let the dough rise as the recipe dictates. If for some reason you cannot bake it when you expected, punch the dough down and just let it rise again. If you need to do this more than once, place the dough in the refrigerator. When you are ready to bake the dough, simply let it come back up to room temperature. Allowing the dough to continue rising can result in the yeast running out of fuel. You will know this has happened if the dough has an acidic bitter smell instead of the homey yeasty aroma, or if the dough had a grayish liquid around the edges of the bowl.

Eastern European Honey Cake with Lemon Sugar Glaze

When I was young and very interested in cooking, a family friend gave me *Betty Crocker's International Cookbook*. It was 1980, and for a girl from a small midwestern town, this book was absolutely exotic! I pored over it with my friend Renee and chose a menu of chicken curry, fried rice, and honey cake. So much for fine thematic cooking. Despite the fact that we worked the entire day and the kitchen was trashed, we were thrilled with the process and the outcome.

This is a dense, intensely flavored cake. I recommend serving it with chicken paprikash or a hearty beef dish, not curry, as I did 25 years ago.

SERVES 10 TO 12

CAKE

3 cups flour

1½ teaspoons baking powder

1 teaspoon baking soda

½ teaspoon salt

1 teaspoon cinnamon

½ teaspoon ginger

½ teaspoon nutmeg or mace

2 teaspoons instant coffee or espresso powder

1 cup sugar

1 cup honey

½ cup vegetable oil

4 eggs

1 tablespoon finely grated lemon peel

3 tablespoons lemon juice

2 tablespoons brandy

⅔ cup cold water

¾ cup chopped walnuts

½ cup raisins

GLAZE

¾ cup sugar

⅓ cup fresh lemon juice

Preheat oven to 350°F. Prepare a 12-cup Bundt pan using butter and flour or Baker's Joy and set aside.

Combine dry ingredients and set aside. Beat sugar, honey, oil, eggs, lemon peel, lemon juice, and brandy in large bowl on medium for 2 minutes. Alternately add the flour mixture and the water to the honey mixture, mixing thoroughly between additions. Beat for 2 minutes at high speed. Fold in the nuts and raisins. Pour into the prepared pan.

Bake for 1 hour to 1 hour 10 minutes, or until a toothpick comes out of the cake clean. Let cool in pan for 10 minutes, and then turn onto a serving plate.

To prepare the Lemon Sugar glaze, mix ¾ cup of sugar with ⅛ cup fresh lemon juice. Place in saucepan and heat until sugar dissolves and the mixture is slightly thickened. Prick top of cake gently with a fork and drizzle with glaze, allowing it to soak in before adding more.

I like to serve this with nuts scattered on the platter. It also looks elegant as a composed dessert with thinly sliced fresh figs and pears fanned around the cake. Or try this with a soft cheese like Humboldt fog, drunken goat, or sharp brie. The blending of savory and sweet with a cup of espresso is a very graceful ending to a formal dinner party.

 A DAUGHTER'S EYES

"I love to play scrabble and recently looked in the dictionary to see if 'Bundt' was an acceptable word. It was, indeed, listed and defined as a 'kind of cake.' It had never occurred to me before that my Dad had invented a new word."

Corrine Dalquist Lynch, daughter of Bundt developers, H. David Dalquist and Dorothy Dalquist

Green Chili Cornbread

An outstanding cornbread that is stunning when cooked in a Bundt pan. Both sweet and savory, it works well with a hearty chili or a platter of jambalaya. I once served it with scrambled eggs cooked with soft cheese and platter of chorizo. Delicious! Feel free to use jalapeños instead of green chilies if you like more of a kick.

SERVES 8 TO 10

1¼ cup all-purpose flour

1 cup yellow cornmeal

3 teaspoons baking powder

½ teaspoon salt

1 cup butter, melted

1 cup white sugar

3 eggs

1 (15-ounce) can cream-style corn

1 (4-ounce) can chopped green chili
    peppers, drained

½ cup shredded Monterey Jack cheese

½ cup shredded Cheddar cheese

Preheat oven to 300°F. Prepare a 12-cup Bundt pan using butter and flour or Baker's Joy and set aside.

Combine flour, cornmeal, baking powder, and salt, and set aside. In a large bowl, beat together butter and sugar until light and pale. Beat in eggs one at a time. Blend in creamed corn, chilies, and the cheeses. Add dry ingredients and mix until blended. Pour the batter into the prepared pan.

Bake for 1 hour or until a toothpick inserted into center of the pan comes out clean. Drizzle the warm cornbread Bundt with butter and a sprinkling of ground chilies.

"AND WHEN I CANNOT WRITE A POEM, I BAKE BISCUITS AND FEEL JUST AS PLEASED." ANNE MORROW LINDBERG, *GIFT FROM THE SEA* (1941)

Orange Pecan Beer Cake with Orange Glaze

Yes, beer. The addition of beer gives this cake a nice, light crumb. The cake is the creation of Julie Rice, who won a Crisco baking contest with it. (I prefer using butter rather than Crisco, but it works fine either way). She advised using a full-flavored dark beer such as Summit Great Northern Porter, and I agree. This is an impressive cake, bursting with the bright tang of orange juice and peel, and the earthy flavor of toasted pecans.

SERVES 10 TO 12

CAKE

3 cups flour

1½ teaspoon baking powder

1½ teaspoon baking soda

¾ cup butter, softened

1½ cups sugar

3 eggs

1½ teaspoons grated orange peel

1 tablespoon orange juice, plus beer
   to make ⅓ cup

1½ cups sour cream

½ teaspoon vanilla extract

FILLING

1 cup chopped pecans, toasted

½ cup sugar

1½ teaspoons grated orange peel

¼ teaspoon nutmeg

¼ teaspoon vanilla

GLAZE

1 orange, peel and juice

⅓ cup light brown sugar

1 tablespoon butter

⅓ cup toasted pecan halves

Preheat the oven to 350°F. Prepare a 12-cup Bundt pan using butter and flour or Baker's Joy and set aside.

For filling, combine chopped pecans, sugar, orange peel, nutmeg, and vanilla. Cover and set aside. For cake, combine flour, baking powder, and baking soda and set aside. Beat butter and sugar until light and fluffy. Add eggs one at a time, beating well after each addition. Beat in orange peel, orange juice and beer mixture, sour cream, and vanilla until smooth. Add the flour mixture and stir only until smooth. Pour ⅓ of the batter into the prepared pan. Top with ⅓ of the filling. Continue in thirds, ending with the filling.

Bake for 45 to 50 minutes or until a toothpick comes out of the cake clean. Cool for 10 minutes in pan and then invert onto a serving platter.

To prepare the glaze, remove peel (without pith) from the orange in long strips and set aside. Combine juice of the orange, sugar, and butter in a small sauce-pan. Heat and gently simmer for about 10 minutes or until the mixture is slightly thickened. Remove from the heat and add the pecans. Brush glaze on top and sides of warm cake, arranging the orange peel and pecans decoratively on top.

"I FEEL THE END APPROACHING. QUICK, BRING ME MY DESSERT, COFFEE AND LIQUEUR."

ANTHELEME BRILLAT-SAVARIN, *THE PHYSIOLOGY OF TASTE* (1825)

Two Moons Wild Rice Bundt with Maple Glaze

In 2006, the Nordic Ware Company sponsored a Bundt contest to celebrate its 60th anniversary. The panel of judges selected a winner from each state and awarded prizes to their favorite ten Bundts. Linda Peterson from Minnesota made it into the Top 10 category with this recipe, and rightfully so! This beautiful and delicious cake celebrates the bounty of Minnesota by combining wild rice, blueberries, maple sugar, and maple syrup. It is wonderful eating in the summer when blueberries are plentiful. I recommend using hand-harvested wild rice, not commercially grown patty rice. A friend of mine, who has been harvesting wild rice for over 50 years, said that real wild rice tastes like your mother's love and the prettiest lake you've ever seen.

SERVES 10 TO 12

CAKE

2¾ cups flour

3 teaspoons baking powder

1 teaspoon salt

⅓ cup butter, softened

⅔ cup sugar

2 large eggs, lightly beaten

1 cup maple syrup

½ cup buttermilk

¾ cup cooled, well-cooked
    and drained wild rice

1 cup fresh blueberries

GLAZE

¾ cup confectioners' sugar

4 to 5 tablespoons maple syrup

2 teaspoons maple sugar

Preheat oven to 350°F. Prepare a 12-cup Bundt pan with butter and flour or Baker's Joy and set aside.

Combine flour, baking powder, and salt and set aside. Beat butter and sugar until fluffy. Add eggs and mix thoroughly. Beat in the maple syrup. Alternately add the flour mixture and the buttermilk to the beaten butter. Stir in wild rice. Gently stir in the wild blueberries. Pour into the prepared pan.

Bake for 50 to 60 minutes or until done. Cool for 10 minutes and invert onto a serving platter.

To prepare the glaze, combine the confectioners' sugar and maple syrup. Drizzle it over the warm cake, then sprinkle the maple sugar over the glaze. Although it may be gilding the lily, the cake is extra delicious served with maple whipped cream (page 137).

 KEEPIN' IT REAL WITH THE ANISHINAABE

The Anishinaabe (Ojibwe) plant and grow several varieties of wild rice and collect it during Manoominike-Giikis, the Wild Rice Moon. Unlike large growers who farm diked paddies in California—where three-quarters of our country's "wild rice" is grown—the Anishinaabe do not grow rice originating with one genetic strand of rice, do not rely on chemicals or fertilizers, and do not use water taken from other ecosytems. Minnesota is one of the few places in the world where true wild rice is grown.

Coming Out Bundt

A friend, after much deliberation, decided to come out at work as gay and in so doing inspired me to make this rainbow Bundt. This cake is magical, because the colored batter reveals itself in two ways: a peek down the center shows the layers of the pride flag, but a cut slice reveals not layers but swirls of color that have gently mingled in the oven. The swirls are never exactly the same each time I bake this, but they are always impressive. Here is a cake worthy of the celebration of someone coming home to themselves and the people around them. So "come out come out wherever you are!" and make this Bundt.

Incidentally, this Bundt will also make most eight-year-olds ecstatic on their birthday! It just screams fun and over-the-top excess.

SERVES 10 TO 12

CAKE

1 (18-ounce) butter white cake
   mix (not yellow!)

1 small box instant French
   vanilla pudding mix

1 cup water

½ cup sour cream or plain yogurt

½ cup melted butter

4 eggs

Liquid food coloring—
   red, blue, and yellow

GLAZE

Juice of 1 large orange

Juice of 1 lemon

½ cup sugar

pinch of salt

Preheat oven to 350°F. Prepare a 12-cup Bundt pan using butter and flour or Baker's Joy and set aside.

Stir together cake mix and pudding mix in a large bowl, making sure to break up any clumps. Make a well in the center and pour in water, sour cream, butter, and eggs. Beat on low speed until blended. Scrape bowl, and beat 4 minutes on medium speed.

Divide the batter evenly into 7 bowls. Add food coloring to each bowl so that you create the following colors: red, orange, yellow, green, blue, purple. (One bowl remains uncolored.) You want fairly vibrant colors, so start with about 15 drops of food coloring in each bowl. Since most packs of food coloring contain only primary colors (red, blue, and yellow), create the other colors this way:

Orange	10 drops of yellow, 5 drops of red
Green	7 drops of yellow, 7 drops of blue
Purple	7 drops of red, 7 drops of blue

Pour half of the uncolored batter into the bottom of the prepared pan. Layer the colors in one at a time in the following order: red, orange, yellow, green, blue, purple. Place the remaining uncolored batter on top. Make the layers as even as possible.

Bake in the preheated oven for 45–50 minutes or until a toothpick inserted into the center of the cake comes out clean. Let cool in pan for 10 minutes, then turn out onto a plate to cool completely.

To prepare glaze, combine orange juice, lemon juice, sugar, and salt in a saucepan. Bring mixture to a boil and then gently simmer until thickened, about 8 minutes. Spoon the lemon-orange syrup on the warm cake. It needs no other adornment!

"PEOPLE WONDER WHY GAYS WANT TO GET MARRIED. IT'S BECAUSE WE WANT OUR OWN DELUXE BUNDT PANS, PEOPLE. JUST SIMPLE AMERICAN THINGS."

HANK STUEVER, *WASHINGTON POST*, JANUARY 11, 2005

Strawberry Pretzel Bundt

I enjoy the fact that Midwesterners often refer to certain gelatin dishes as salads. People in other parts of the country *do not* do this; they hold onto the notion that a salad involves greens or, at least, vegetables and does not include Cool Whip. Well, call this whatever you like, but make it. This Bundt is gorgeous and offers the perfect balance of sweet, savory-crunchy, and creamy.

I adapted this recipe from one given to me by my friend Erin, whose family embodies the best of what it means to be Minnesotan. They are kind and progressive-thinking people, but also a bit wacky. They invited me to their annual family "talent show" at Christmas even when I barely knew them, and, thankfully, nearly any human activity met their definition of talent. Erin's cousin Lois made gelatin for the event several years in a row, and this recipe was the family's favorite. I adapted it for the Bundt pan and cut down a little on its sweetness. This Bundt works beautifully at a Christmas buffet supper or a 1970s disco bash.

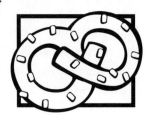

SERVES 10 TO 12

1½ cups crushed pretzels (mini stick pretzels work best)

4 tablespoons, plus ½ cup, sugar

10 tablespoons butter, melted

1 (8-ounce) package cream cheese

1 cup heavy cream or 4 ounces of whipped topping, thawed

1 large (6-ounce) box of strawberry-flavored gelatin

2 cups boiling water

1 (16-ounce) package frozen sliced strawberries

Lightly oil a 12-cup Bundt pan and set aside. Preheat the oven to 350°F.

Mix together the pretzels, 4 tablespoons sugar, and melted butter. It will look quite buttery; that is fine. Press into the bottom of the prepared Bundt pan. Bake for 10 to 12 minutes, or until lightly toasted. Set aside to cool completely.

In a medium bowl, beat ½ cup sugar and cream cheese until smooth. If you are using the heavy cream, prepare the stabilized version found on page 137. Fold this or the commercially prepared whipped topping into the cream cheese mixture. Spread evenly over the cooled crust. The more evenly this is spread, the more beautiful your Bundt will be. Refrigerate until set, about 45 minutes.

In a medium bowl, stir together the gelatin mix and boiling water. Mix in frozen strawberries, and stir until thawed. You may have to break up clumps with a metal fork. Pour into pan over cream cheese mixture. If you have a little left, pour it into a serving dish and use for another purpose. Refrigerate until completely chilled, at least 2 hours.

Just prior to serving, dip the Bundt into a large bowl of warm water, taking care not to allow water into pan. Run a sharp knife gently around the edge of the pan and the center hole. Invert onto a serving platter. No additional adornments necessary!

Glazes

Almond Glaze

Apricot Glaze

Chili Glaze

Chocolate Glaze

Cider Glaze

Cinnamon Glaze

Espresso Glaze

Honey Butter Glaze

Lemon Glaze

Lemon-Orange Syrup

Lime Syrup

Maple Glaze

Orange Glaze

Almond Glaze

Great taste on a Glazed Almond Bundt Cake (page 54) or Sour Cream Coffee Cake (page 52).

¼ cup milk
¾ cup sugar
½ teaspoon almond extract
½ cup sliced almonds, toasted

Place all of the ingredients in a saucepan and bring to a boil. Reduce the heat and stir until sugar is dissolved and the mixture is slightly thickened. Pour the topping over a warm cake and serve warm or at room temperature.

Apricot Glaze

Good with Apricot Almond Pound Cake (page 36).

1 cup apricot preserves
Juice of ½ lemon
½ cup water

In a small saucepan combine ½ cup of apricot preserves, lemon juice, and water. Bring to a boil and beat until combined and the larger apricot pieces have broken into smaller bits. The glaze should be slightly thickened, but thin enough to pour. If it is too thick, add more water. If it is too thin, cook longer. Spoon or brush the glaze over a hot cake, taking care to cover it thoroughly.

Chili Glaze

Serve with Pine Nut and Chili Bundt Cake (page 104).

Juice of 1 lemon
2 tablespoons sugar
1 tablespoon honey
1 teaspoon ground chilies

Place lemon juice, sugar, honey, and ground chilies in a saucepan and bring to a boil. Reduce the heat and continue cooking until the mixture thickens, about 4 minutes. Spoon or brush a cake with the glaze and serve slightly warm or at room temperature.

 GROUND CHILIES

Many recipes in southwestern cooking call for ground red chilies. Although they may look similar to chili powder, chilies are an entirely different beast. The familiar American chili powder, which contains salt, MSG, and other spices, should never be substituted for ground chilies.

Ground chilies are exactly what the words say, finely ground red chilies. Although many chili varieties are used, chilies from Chimayo, New Mexico, are among the very best. They are available at most Mexican grocery stores or online.

Chocolate Glaze

A shiny glaze that puts a beautiful sheen on nearly any Bundt cake. It is sweet, but thin so that it does not overwhelm the cake. Although it is at its best when made with high-quality chocolate, I have also had good results with Nestlé's chocolate chips.

½ cup cream
2 tablespoons corn syrup
pinch of salt
1 cup chocolate pieces or chips (bittersweet or semi-sweet are best)

Place all ingredients in a small saucepan and simmer over medium heat, stirring constantly until the chocolate is melted and the mixture is smooth. Cool for 15 to 20 minutes, stirring occasionally until the glaze is thickened, but still pourable. Drizzle on cake.

Cider Glaze

Good with Apple Butter Bundt (page 72).

1 cup apple cider (not apple juice)
2 tablespoons honey
Juice of ½ lemon

½ cup sugar
½ cup confectioners' sugar
½ teaspoon cornstarch

Place apple cider, honey, lemon juice, and sugar in a small saucepan. Bring it to a rolling boil. Reduce the heat to maintain a low boil and stir constantly until the mixture thickens slightly, about 5 minutes. Remove 2 tablespoons of the cider mixture and thoroughly dissolve the cornstarch in it. Return it to the saucepan and continue to cook until mixture thickens further, about 4 minutes. Add ½ cup confectioners' sugar and cook until the glaze is thick enough to be spooned over the cake, about 4 minutes.

Brush glaze over the hot cake. This process will use about ⅔ of the glaze. When the cake is cooled, spoon the remaining glaze over the cake. It will have thickened considerably giving it the appearance of honey.

Cinnamon Glaze

Serve this on Bubble Loaf (page 40) or Cinnamon Swirl Coffee Cake (page 46).

½ cup sugar

1 cup chopped pecans

¼ cup melted butter

1 teaspoon cinnamon

¼ cup corn syrup

Combine the sugar, pecans, butter, cinnamon, and corn syrup in a small saucepan and heat gently until the sugar is dissolved and the mixture is thoroughly combined. Pour the glaze over the inverted loaf and serve. Although it is delicious at room temperature, it really shines when you serve it warm.

Espresso Glaze

Terrific on Express Chocolate Espresso Bundt (page 14) or Chocolate Pound Cake (page 22).

¾ cup confectioners' sugar
3 tablespoons strongly brewed coffee
2 teaspoons instant espresso powder

Combine confectioners' sugar, coffee, and espresso powder in a small bowl and beat until smooth. If it is stiff and not pourable, add a bit more coffee. If it is too thin, add a little more confectioners' sugar. Brush or spoon the glaze over the cake while it is still warm.

Honey Butter Glaze

A good all-around topping that eliminates the somewhat dry appearance Bundts can have if they are not frosted or glazed. This glaze is especially useful if you want to serve the Bundt with just a dusting of confectioners' sugar because the cake appears moist and the confectioners' sugar adheres to the surface. This glaze will keep in the refrigerator for two weeks if you store it in an air-tight container.

8 tablespoons butter, softened
6 tablespoons honey, warmed slightly

Beat the butter and honey together until light and fluffy. Allow it to return to room temperature or warm in the microwave for 8 to 10 seconds before using. Beat the honey butter again just before using.

Lemon Glaze

Use with Quick Lemon Poppy Seed Cake (page 38) or Sour Cream Coffee Cake (page 42).

1 tablespoon buttermilk
2 cups confectioners' sugar
2 to 3 tablespoons lemon juice

Whisk together the buttermilk, confectioners' sugar, and 2 tablespoons of lemon juice until smooth. Add the remaining tablespoon of juice if necessary to make it pourable. Pour half of the glaze over the warm cake. Cool 1 hour and pour the remaining glaze over the cake. If you do not want the glaze to pool on the serving platter, apply the glaze to the cake while still on the cooling rack.

Lemon–Orange Syrup

Complements a Cranberry Orange Bundt (page 60) or the Coming Out Bundt (page 116).

Juice of 1 large orange
Juice of 1 lemon
⅓ cup sugar
pinch of salt

Combine orange juice, lemon juice, sugar, and salt in a saucepan. Bring to a boil and then gently simmer until it is thickened, about 8 minutes. Spoon or brush the cake with the hot syrup.

Lime Syrup

This simple but delicious syrup adds zing to many Bundt cakes. It is especially good on pound cake.

Juice of 2 limes
¼ cup water
3 tablespoons sugar
1 tablespoon honey

Place all of the ingredients in a small saucepan and simmer over medium heat until the sugar dissolves and the mixture thickens. You can apply this hot to the cake (and it will soak in and give the cake a very moist exterior) or brush it on at room temperature for a more textured look.

Maple Glaze

Use with Maple Corn Coffee Cake (page 48).

⅓ cup pure maple syrup

Gently heat the maple syrup in the microwave until hot, about 20 seconds. Watch this carefully, because microwave temperatures vary and the syrup can easily boil over. Brush the syrup over the cake, allowing it to soak in before adding more.

Orange Glaze

This is a light, sweet glaze that works well on pound cakes, coffee cakes, and the Quick Orange Kiss (page 92). It is similar to the other citrus glazes, but offers a sweeter, more mellow touch to the Bundt.

Juice of 2 oranges (about 8 tablespoons)
3 tablespoons sugar

Place orange juice and sugar in a small saucepan and simmer over medium heat until the sugar dissolves and the mixture thickens. Apply this hot to the cake (it will soak in and give the cake a very moist exterior) or brush it on at room temperature for a more textured look.

Frostings and Fillings

Butter Vanilla Frosting

Buttercream

Chocolate Buttercream

Coffee Buttercream

Caramel Frosting

Coconut Caramel Filling or Frosting

Cream Cheese Frosting

Fluffy Coconut Frosting

Peanut Butter Frosting

Whipped Cream

Cocoa Whipped Cream

Ginger-Scented Whipped Cream

Maple Whipped Cream

Mock Crème Fraîche Whipped Cream

Butter Vanilla Frosting

This is the lovely frosting your grandma probably made for you when you were little. Adults sometimes claim it is too sweet and then ask for a piece of cake with lots of frosting.

8 tablespoons softened butter

1 egg yolk

2 cups confectioners' sugar

1 teaspoon vanilla

Beat the butter until creamy and light. Stir in the egg yolk and continue beating. Add the sugar a little at a time and continue beating until smooth. Add the vanilla and beat until fluffy.

Buttercream

A recipe from *The Cake Bible* (1988) by Rose Levy Beranbaum, who uses corn syrup to eliminate the need for a candy thermometer and prevent crystallization. Buttercream feels decadent and luxurious because of the amount of butter that goes into it. It will make your Bundt feel and taste very special.

6 egg yolks

¾ cup sugar

½ cup corn syrup

2 cups softened butter

Grease a 1-cup measuring cup and set aside. Beat the yolks in a large bowl until very light in color and set aside. Combine sugar and corn syrup in a saucepan and bring to a rolling boil, stirring constantly. Pour the syrup into the greased measuring cup. Beat the syrup into the yolks with an electric mixer at high speed until the mixture is cool. (Avoid pouring the syrup onto the moving beaters since it will spin it out to the sides of the bowl.) Gradually beat in the butter, a tablespoon at a time until the buttercream is fluffy and light. Use immediately or store in an airtight container in the refrigerator. Return it to room temperature before you use it.

Variations

Chocolate Buttercream: Beat 6 ounces of melted and cooled chocolate into the buttercream. Use high-quality dark or bittersweet chocolate for best results.

Coffee Buttercream: Dissolve 2 tablespoons of instant espresso powder into hot black coffee or boiling water. Beat this into the finished buttercream.

Caramel Frosting

This sweet, rich frosting goes well with chocolate, coconut, or peanut butter cakes. It's the kind of frosting that will cause your family to fight over licking the spoon, bowl, and beaters.

8 tablespoons butter

1 cup brown sugar

¼ teaspoon salt

⅛ cup half-and-half

1 teaspoon vanilla extract

3½ cups confectioners' sugar

Melt the butter in a small saucepan. Stir in brown sugar and salt and cook over medium heat for 3 minutes until sugar is dissolved. Stir in the half-and-half and return to a boil. Remove from the heat and allow it to cool to room temperature. Stir in vanilla and beat in the confectioners' sugar until the frosting is fluffy and spreadable. This recipe will frost generously one Bundt cake.

Coconut Caramel Filling or Frosting

You will recognize this as the familiar filling-frosting used on a German Chocolate Cake (page 26).

1 cup evaporated milk

1 cup sugar

2 egg yolks, slightly beaten

½ cup butter

1 teaspoon vanilla

1½ cups Baker's Angel Flake coconut

1 cup chopped pecans

Mix the evaporated milk, sugar, egg yolks, butter, and vanilla in a saucepan and stir over medium heat until thickened. This should take from 10 to 15 minutes depending on heat and humidity. Stir in the coconut and nuts. Cool until it is thick enough to spread.

Cream Cheese Frosting

This classic frosting is good with nearly every Bundt you'll want to make. Make sure that the cream cheese is at room temperature before you begin. If you are in a pinch, pre-heat your oven to 180°F. Turn off the oven and put the cream cheese in a metal bowl in the oven. It will be soft enough to use in about 5 minutes.

8 ounces cream cheese, softened

⅓ cup butter, softened

2 cups confectioners' sugar

1½ teaspoon vanilla extract

Combine all of the ingredients in a food processor or electric mixer and beat until smooth and fluffy. Frost the Bundt.

Fluffy Coconut Frosting

This light frosting makes an attractive Bundt Cake. It is really just a simple butter frosting with cream and coconut added to it. The frosting also works nicely with cupcakes.

10 tablespoons butter, softened

1 egg yolk

2 cups confectioners' sugar

3 to 4 tablespoons half-and-half

⅜ cup flake coconut

Beat the butter until creamy and light. Stir in the egg yolk and continue beating. Add the sugar a little at a time and continue beating until smooth. Add the half-and-half and beat until very fluffy. A balloon whisk attachment on a freestanding mixer works very well for this. Stir in the coconut.

KEEP IT SIMPLE

I saw a Cathedral Bundt at a potluck that was covered in 2 inches of buttercream. The cake was delicious, but all that frosting obscured its beauty. Complicated or ornate Bundt forms demand simple glazes or toppings added at the table.

Peanut Butter Frosting

Use this with the Peanut Butter and Jelly Bundt (page 66) or a Chocolate Peanut-Butter Chip Bundt (page 20).

¼ cup butter, softened
⅓ cup smooth peanut butter
1 teaspoon vanilla
2 cups sifted confectioners' sugar
3 to 4 tablespoons half-and-half

Cream the butter until fluffy. Add the peanut butter and vanilla and combine thoroughly. Add the sugar alternating with the half-and half-until light and fluffy. Frost your Bundt.

Whipped Cream

Adding whipped cream to your kitchen repertoire is a wise move. Whipped cream is versatile, delicious, and can be ready in minutes. The worst that can happen is that you accidentally make butter, and how bad can that be? I have been amazed at the number of people I've met who have never had real whipped cream! One young woman at our church said to me, "I thought whipped cream came in a tub or a spray can!" She was quite impressed with her first taste of the real thing. People will practically eat roadkill if it has real whipped cream on it.

Stabilized whipped cream (page 137) makes it easier to prepare the cream ahead. Without the stabilizing power of cornstarch, whipped cream can "water out" and mar the flavor and appearance of the Bundt.

1 cup heavy whipping cream
2 tablespoons sugar (more if you like your whipped cream sweeter)

Place the cream and sugar in a mixing bowl and chill for at least 20 minutes. Make sure to chill the beaters too. If you want to fill your Bundt with cream, beat until stiff peaks form. If you want to mound the cream on top of the Bundt or serve it on the side, beat until soft peaks form. Fill or top your Bundt and refrigerate it for an hour.

Variations

Cocoa Whipped Cream: Add 3 tablespoons of cocoa powder to the cream before whipping it.

Ginger-Scented Whipped Cream: Add 1 to 2 teaspoons of ginger powder to the cream before whipping it. I prefer this method to using fresh ginger, since fresh ginger's high acid content interferes with whipping the cream.

Maple Whipped Cream: Add 2 to 3 tablespoons of pure maple syrup instead of sugar to the cream before whipping it.

Mock Crème Fraîche Whipped Cream: This is nice when you want a bit of tang in your whipped cream. Simply add ⅛ cup sour cream and beat as above.

 PREPARING STABILIZED WHIPPED CREAM AHEAD

To keep whipped cream from separating, stabilize it. Instead of mixing sugar into the whipping cream, add 1 teaspoon of cornstarch and 2 tablespoons of confectioners' sugar to ¼ cup of whipping cream. Bring to a boil and simmer until slightly thickened. Allow the mixture to cool and add it to the remaining ¾ cup of cream. Beat as above and refrigerate until it is time to frost your cake.

Sauces

Butterscotch Sauce

Coconut Cream Lime Sauce

Lemon Curd

Old-Fashioned Lemon Sauce

Raspberry Rhubarb Sauce

Butterscotch Sauce

An easy-to-prepare sauce that makes any Bundt cake feel and taste special. Rich and luxurious, it will keep in the refrigerator for up to two weeks.

1 cup brown sugar

½ cup butter

½ cup heavy cream

1 teaspoon vanilla extract

1 teaspoon bourbon

Combine brown sugar, butter, and cream in a small saucepan and cook over medium heat until the sugar dissolves and the mixture thickens slightly. This takes about 8 to 10 minutes. Remove from the heat and whisk in the vanilla and bourbon. The sauce will thicken as it cools to room temperature.

Coconut Cream Lime Sauce

I developed this sauce for a dinner party when I wanted to serve East Indian food, but knew that one guest would want a "traditional" dessert. The sauce is also good with the addition of fresh ginger, which gives it a little zing!

½ can coconut milk (available in the Asian section of most grocery stores)

⅓ cup sugar

1 tablespoon cornstarch

1 teaspoon rum

1 teaspoon vanilla extract

1 tablespoon butter

½ teaspoon grated fresh ginger (optional)

Place the coconut milk and sugar in a small saucepan. Cook on medium heat, stirring constantly until the sugar is dissolved. Add the cornstarch and continue cooking until mixture thickens. Remove from heat and stir in rum, vanilla, butter, and, if desired, ginger. (Freezing ginger, by the way, is an easy way to avoid a watery, fibrous mess when grating.) Cool to room temperature, and spoon on each individual piece of cake.

Lemon Curd

This makes an elegant accompaniment to many Bundt cakes. It is also useful as a way to rescue a cake that has stuck to the pan and cannot be easily patched.

4 eggs
Zest of 2 large or 3 small lemons
7 tablespoons of lemon juice
1 cup of sugar
8 tablespoons of butter

Place the eggs in a small bowl and beat until thoroughly blended. Set aside. Place the zest, juice, sugar, and butter in the top of a double boiler or in a metal bowl suspended over hot water. Do not let the bowl touch the water. Stir until the butter melts and the sugar dissolves. Spoon about ⅛ cup of the hot mixture into the eggs and beat until blended. Add this back to the hot mixture and continue cooking and stirring over the hot water until the mixture is thoroughly cooked and thickened. Remove from heat. Remove any large pieces of egg white that may have thickened and become unsightly. Cool thoroughly and refrigerate until ready to use.

Old-Fashioned Lemon Sauce

This old recipe allowed people to enjoy the flavor of lemon at a time when they could not get fresh lemons. This sauce is delicious served warm, but is also good at room temperature spooned over a lemon or pound cake.

1 tablespoon cornstarch

3 tablespoons plus 1½ cups water

⅔ cup brown sugar

¼ teaspoon salt

2 tablespoons butter

¾ teaspoon lemon extract

Dissolve cornstarch in the 3 tablespoons of water and set aside. Mix 1½ cups water, brown sugar, salt, and butter in a saucepan and bring to a boil. Add cornstarch mixture and stir constantly until the sauce is smooth and thickened, about 3 minutes. Remove from heat and stir in lemon extract.

Raspberry Rhubarb Sauce

I could eat a bowl of this in one sitting. Okay, I have eaten a bowl of this in one sitting. It is a wonderful blend of sweet and tart and looks lovely on a coffee or pound cake. Feel free to substitute strawberries or blueberries for the raspberries if that's what you have on hand. It will keep well in the refrigerator for up to one week.

2 cups chopped rhubarb

1 cup fresh or frozen raspberries

½ cup water

½ cup sugar (more or less depending on your preference)

Juice of ½ lemon

Combine all of the ingredients in a saucepan and simmer over medium heat until the rhubarb breaks down and the sugar is dissolved. This typically takes 10 to 12 minutes. Allow the sauce to come to room temperature before using it.

Index